Why Do Teachers Need to Know about Child Development?

Why Do Teachers Need to Know about Child Development?

Strengthening Professional Identity and Well-Being

**Edited by
Daryl Maisey and
Verity Campbell-Barr**

BLOOMSBURY ACADEMIC
LONDON • NEW YORK • OXFORD • NEW DELHI • SYDNEY

BLOOMSBURY ACADEMIC
Bloomsbury Publishing Plc
50 Bedford Square, London, WC1B 3DP, UK
1385 Broadway, New York, NY 10018, USA
29 Earlsfort Terrace, Dublin 2, Ireland

BLOOMSBURY, BLOOMSBURY ACADEMIC and the Diana logo
are trademarks of Bloomsbury Publishing Plc

First published in Great Britain, 2021

Cover design by Charlotte James
Cover image © naqiewei/ iStock

A catalogue record for this book is available from the British Library.

Library of Congress Cataloging-in-Publication Data
Names: Maisey, Daryl, editor. | Campbell-Barr, Verity, editor.
Title: Why Do Teachers Need to Know about Child Development?: Strengthening Professional
Identity and Well-Being / Edited by Daryl Maisey and Verity Campbell-Barr.
Description: London; New York: Bloomsbury Academic, 2021. |
Series: Personal, social and emotional perspectives for educators |
Includes bibliographical references and index.
Identifiers: LCCN 2020036907 (print) | LCCN 2020036908 (ebook) |
ISBN 9781350084940 (hardback) | ISBN 9781350084933 (paperback) |
ISBN 9781350084957 (epub) | ISBN 9781350084964 (ebook)
Subjects: LCSH: Child development. | School children–Psychology. | Teacher-student relationships.
Classification: LCC LB1115 .W58 2021 (print) | LCC LB1115 (ebook) | DDC 372.21–dc23
LC record available at https://lccn.loc.gov/2020036907
LC ebook record available at ttps://lccn.loc.gov/2020036908

ISBN: HB: 978-1-3500-8494-0
         PB: 978-1-3500-8493-3
         ePDF: 978-1-3500-8496-4
         ePUB: 978-1-3500-8495-7

Series: Personal, Social and Emotional Perspectives for Educators

Typeset by Integra Software Services Pvt. Ltd.
Printed and bound in Great Britain

To find out more about our authors and books visit www.bloomsbury.com
and sign up for our newsletters.

To educators everywhere – embrace your inner penguin!

Contents

Series Editor's Preface

The textbooks in the *Personal, Social and Emotional Perspective for Educators* series are explicitly designed to support teachers in establishing and developing an holistic understanding of a teacher's role and responsibilities in the twenty-first century. They specifically aim to help trainee, beginning and experienced teachers gain both confidence and knowledge in their professional role working with pupils from the early years through to university entrance. Each book asks the question '*Why do teachers need to know about …* ' and is focused on a different area of pedagogy crucial for modern-day teaching practice, providing a breadth of perspectives about teaching and learning. Importantly, in conjunction with this they provide practice examples and searching questions which challenge readers to consider their own views, beliefs and values, on child development, special, able and talented and dual exceptionality and psychology. This innovative book series gives teachers the opportunity and space to develop an enhanced understanding of their role and the professional self.

Recognizing the importance of both practice and theory every chapter is co-authored by a teacher practitioner from various stages of schooling and an education academic, enabling real-life cases from around the world to be discussed alongside theoretical and research-based studies. Although chapter titles will differ between the books the same topics of discussion will be critically explored in most cases. These will consider the importance of the professional self, health and well-being, outdoor education, technology, listening to pupils and reflective practice.

My editorial colleagues and I hope this book series will provide you with a clear sense of the significance and value of the teacher's role and the art of inclusive teaching for all pupils. Teaching is without doubt a demanding and all-encompassing profession, but with resilience and a continuing willingness to learn and adapt, it is one of the most rewarding.

Dr Sue Soan
Series Editor

Series Editor's Introduction to the *Personal, Social and Emotional Perspectives for Educators* Series

This is a textbook trilogy which will help trainee, beginning and experienced teachers gain confidence and knowledge in working with pupils aged two through to nineteen (and perhaps even beyond). Unlike other texts it provides teachers with the opportunity to consider their practice not only from the perspective of strategies or interventions used and curricula engaged with, but also through a holistic examination of their professional role and responsibilities.

The titles of the book series *Personal, Social and Emotional Perspectives for Educators* are:

> *Why Do Teachers Need to Know about Child Development?*
> *Why Do Teachers Need to Know about Diverse Learning Needs?*
> *Why Do Teachers Need to Know about Psychology?*

The series aims to enable every teacher to see why and how it is essential they recognize their own personal, social and emotional responsibilities when educating their pupils. It is for this reason the titles of each book ask a question. The editors consider it is important for all teachers to consistently ask the question 'why?' from their own personal perspective as well as from a professional perspective. Without this ongoing reflection and reflexivity, practice can become 'stale' and views 'fixed'. Twenty-first-century life is not static, but constantly changing and throwing humankind unexpected challenges, requiring professionals and leaders to be flexible, well-informed change-agents and open to new knowledge. But, of course, it is no use asking 'why?' if the 'how' and 'what' are neglected because without a focus on these types of questions as well teachers will not know what needs to change or how to change them. Thus, throughout the series, answers to the 'why?' questions are given through exploration of the 'what and how,' enabling teachers the opportunity to develop a deep understanding of how they can enhance their practice and as a consequence maintain motivation and enhance their resilience and expertise.

The books are written with an international audience in mind and hope to support all teachers around the world whatever their context or pupil age group. The decision was made that the term 'pupil' would be used to try and avoid confusion between school pupils and teacher trainees or students. This generic term also facilitated avoiding the often, artificial boundaries teachers and other educators put around practice for different age groups. All children and young people, whatever their age, learning, social or emotional needs, are therefore called pupils. It is hoped that no-one is offended by this decision and if so, that was not the intention. All actual names used in chapters have been altered to maintain anonymity unless specific written agreement has been obtained stating that their name or the name of an institution can be used. Of course, language has not been altered in any quotations, in the Window on research or Case studies and 'child' or 'children' is used when parental perspectives are offered.

Whichever book in the series is picked up first readers will find that all authors examine, through the subject content, what it means to be a 'teacher'. They consider not only aspects such as the professional self, but also the role of reflection and reflexivity in developing an understanding of the self and the day-to-day experiences in teaching. For clarity, *reflection* is defined in the books as the action of personal purposeful thinking about education to improve professional practice. *Reflexivity* involves 'question[ing] our own attitudes, theories-in-use, values, assumptions, prejudices and habitual actions; to understand our complex roles in relation to others' (Bolton and Delderfield, 2018:10 in Chapter 8 of *Why Do Teachers Need to Know about Diverse Learning Needs?*). As Codina and Fordham (2021:120, in Soan, 2021:119–136) state 'a teacher's reflexive awareness should therefore shape their in-action reflections; i.e. the in the moment choices teachers make concerning interactions with others (colleagues, parents, children).'

Recognizing the significance of connecting theory to practice and vice versa, each chapter (with the exception of chapter 1 in *Why Do Teachers Need to Know about Diverse Learning Needs?*) is co-written by a teacher practitioner and an education academic. This enables the welding together of practice experience and knowledge, and theoretical and research evidence, rather than just providing a passing glance from one arena to the other.

Finally, it is anticipated that these books will provide teachers at all stages of their professional career with the information and challenge required for them to see the significance and value of the teacher role and the art of teaching for all pupils whatever their learning or developmental needs. Humankind needs teachers now more than ever who can motivate, capture their pupils' interests and abilities, and challenge them to always ask questions and seek answers. Teaching can be without doubt the most fulfilling profession when fully understood, and it is suggested that as a natural consequence of this every pupil then becomes inclusively taught, valued and nurtured.

Dr Sue Soan
Series Editor

Using This Book

Each book follows a similar structure. Due to its professional parameters and distinctive focus, *Why Do Teachers Need to Know about Child Development?* considers technology and learning environments within chapters rather than having specific chapters on these topics. Each chapter is designed to critically explore different subject areas. These are reflected across the trilogy and are considered important to professional development today and include:

- The professional self
- Health and well-being
- The learning environment
- Technology
- Listening
- Professional relationships and collaboration
- Resilience, reflection, reflexivity
- The role of the teacher

Within each chapter

Each chapter includes a number of features to make connections between theory and practice explicit and alive, drawing on experiences and research from a range of settings:

 Case studies   Window on research

 Window on practice   Reflective questions

 Reflexive questions

Each chapter ends with an Annotated bibliography.

At the end of the book

In order to also support busy educators, trainees and teachers, all of the references, whilst placed together towards the end of the book, are listed in chapter order.

Editors

Daryl Maisey is Associate Professor in the Department of Education at Kingston University, UK. She originally trained as a primary school teacher and gained over twenty years of experience working across the primary and early years sectors of education. When Daryl moved into Higher Education, she was involved in programme developments to enable opportunities for education practitioners to continue working whilst studying, and this commitment to work-based learning remains one of her key interests. Daryl currently teaches on the Master of Research (Education) and PGCE programmes. Her research interests include early years, safeguarding and child protection and interprofessional practice.

Verity Campbell-Barr is Associate Professor in Early Childhood Studies and Associate Head of Research at Plymouth Institute of Education, University of Plymouth, UK. Verity has over fifteen years of experience researching early childhood education and care services. Her research interests centre on the quality of early childhood services, particularly the role of the early childhood workforce in supporting the quality of services. She has a particular interest in the concept of child-centredness and what it means for quality pedagogic interactions within early years services and has co-led two European projects in this area. Verity has also undertaken international research on the knowledge, skills and attitudes for working in early childhood services and has recently embarked on an analysis of the full range of early childhood degrees available in England. She has written extensively on quality and the workforce in early childhood services and has recently published *Professional Knowledge and Skills in the Early Years*.

Contributors

Julie Berry is currently a full-time Mum. She began working in the Early Years field twenty years ago. She has gained a variety of qualifications and undertaken many courses to enhance her understanding and knowledge within her job roles. Julie completed her BA (Hons) Early Childhood Studies degree at the University of Plymouth, graduating in 2012 with a first class degree. Julie is very passionate about the set-up of Early Years settings in the UK, especially mainstream education. Her dissertation research was based on the role of the Early Years teacher. Her passion is reading around the constant changes and external influences on the educational system and the professional roles within it. This topic and interest has never been more at the fore since having her own child, now of school age.

James Bettany is Lecturer at the University of Plymouth, UK. James grew up in the Cayman Islands, and in his role as an academic at the University of Plymouth his focus is on exploring science and technology in Primary and Early Years' classroom settings with trainee teachers on BEd and PGCE routes into teaching. James qualified as a primary school teacher in 2012, teaching in mainstream and special schools in Plymouth. He completed a Master's degree in learning for sustainability in 2016. This fed an interest in the role of storytelling as a stimulus for dialogue around issues of sustainability. He plans to link these ideas to the related field of ecolinguistics as part of a doctoral study. James has been a consultant on curriculum design for computing in international schools and presented at the BETT show.

Maria Dowling is a health and social care consultant, specializing in inclusive practice. Having previously worked as a provider and commissioning manager within health and social care settings for children and adults with disabilities, Maria also has significant experience within the education sector, both as a mainstream primary teacher and as a Senior Lecturer in Special Educational Needs and Inclusive Practice at Kingston University. Maria's experience of working across health, social care and education sectors enables her to understand the importance of partnership working across disciplines in order to effectively support children and families.

Martin Gilchrist works for Natural England, the UK government's advisory body on the natural environment in England. He has worked as a countryside ranger, community wildlife officer and has been involved in a range of community- and learning-based initiatives to engage people with the natural environment over the last twenty-five years including the Natural Connections Demonstration Project.

Norma Goodyear provides specialist support for inclusion in a primary school. Norma began supporting children in the classroom over twenty years ago and this sparked an interest in increasing her knowledge about how best to support learning for each unique child. She gained the National Professional Qualification for Children's Centre Leaders and this inspired her to study further and achieve a Masters degree in Child Centred Interprofessional Practice at Kingston University. During her career Norma has worked in a variety of children's settings supporting children and their families. Having gained a postgraduate certificate in Specific Learning Difficulties, Norma now works in a primary school providing children with literacy support. In her spare time, she is currently enjoying not having to meet assignment deadlines!

Cheryl Graham is an Early Years Professional with a Degree in Psychology and a Masters in Education. She has thirty years' experience of managing an Early Years Setting – working with children and families from diverse backgrounds, abilities and socio-economic needs. Her working practice is influenced by holistic approaches, such as Te Whāriki, and the importance of understanding how cultural and social influences shape children's early experiences. Her research explores whether standardizing the Early Year's curriculum introduces an adult agenda of assessment and targets, and whether this may impact on working practice and how we view and support children in their early years.

Mary Hodson is Senior Lecturer at Kingston University, UK. Following a twenty-year career in psychiatric nursing, Mary re-trained as a primary school teacher in south-west London. After some years in the teaching profession, she successfully completed her MA in Child Centred Interprofessional Practice and moved into Higher Education at Kingston University. Mary is a Fellow of the Higher Education Academy, and her research interests include children and young peoples' voices, suicide and self-harm in schools and the role of liaison working in Higher Education. In her spare time, Mary enjoys relaxing with friends and walking.

Claire Jackson is currently the Course Leader for the Primary PGCE programme at Kingston University, UK. She has extensive teaching and management experience in a diverse range of schools where she worked in close partnership with other practitioners/teachers, parents and local authorities, before moving into Further and Higher Education. Her current research explores the teaching and assessment of science in early years. Along with her co-researcher, Claire developed a model and tool for assessing science (FASEY) which is being trialled in partnership with a London school. The research focuses on enquiry-based, collaborative learning through play. Claire is also passionate about outdoor learning and has a level 3 Forest School Advanced Leader qualification. Claire leads Forest School sessions in nurseries and schools and is currently developing the Forest School site and provision at Kingston University to enable sessions for local schools, facilitated by Education and Social Work students. Claire's other areas of interest and expertise include child development, creativity and engaging children in decision making.

Jessica Johnson was Senior Lecturer at Kingston University, UK, until she recently retired. Starting her professional career in paediatric nursing and health visiting, Jessica's ongoing interest in ways to build positive, trusting relationships for children and adults has developed across disciplines over time, including the voluntary sector and education. As a senior lecturer at Kingston University, she developed and taught programmes that acknowledged inter-professional practice and research. As a primary school governor, she remains engaged with safeguarding policies and practice, health and well-being strategies and staff development. Volunteering with a local Riding for the Disabled group provides ongoing opportunities to extend her range of language and communication skills. She continues to learn through play and hands-on care with an ever-increasing number of grandchildren!

Rowena Passy is Senior Research Fellow at the Plymouth Institute of Education, University of Plymouth, UK, where she moved in 2010 from employment as a Senior Research Officer at the National Foundation for Education Research. She has a long-standing interest in learning outdoors, and was Evaluation Manager for the Natural Connections Demonstration Project 2012–16. She is now involved in the Erasmus+ project Go Out and Learn that aims to develop cross-cultural approaches to outdoor learning and is supporting Public Health Dorset with a project that is exploring links between well-being and physical activity. She is Associate Editor of the *Journal of Experiential Education* and is co-leader of Peninsula Research in Outdoor Learning, the south-west regional hub of the National Research Network hosted by the Institute of Outdoor Learning.

Catherine Warnock is Early Years Foundation Stage Leader and Reception Teacher in the UK. Catherine's first career was as a Food Technologist before she worked as a parent volunteer and then as a Teaching Assistant in a Reception class. Inspired by her experience, Catherine undertook a work-based Early Years degree through Kingston University, followed by a PGCE at Froebel College, Roehampton. Catherine has spent the last ten years teaching in both state and independent schools and currently works as EYFS Leader and Reception Teacher in a child-centred, independent school in North London. Her interest in personal resilience and the emotional dimensions of teaching developed as a result of experiences working in a profession undergoing constant change.

Ruth Wood is Associate Professor at Kingston University, UK, and currently teaches on the Master of Research (Education) and the Doctor of Education programmes in the Department of Education. Her research interests involve the pedagogy of educational technology, more specifically, the interface between learner, teacher and the technology including the design and use of multimedia and multimodal forms of communication in a range of education settings. Challenges associated with the design, development and implementation of technological innovations and the potential role of the teacher and learner remain central, active ingredients of her research.

Acknowledgements

Thank you to all of our contributors and their families for supporting them and to Sue for guiding us along the way.

Abbreviations

AAC	Augmentative and Alternative Communication
AIDS	Acquired immunodeficiency syndrome
AfA	Achievement for All
AGT	Able, Gifted and Talented
AR	Augmented Reality
ASC	Autism Spectrum Condition
ASD	Autism Spectrum Disorder
BSL	British Sign Language
ChYPMHS	Children's and Young People Mental Health Services
CPD	Continuing Professional Development
CQC	Care Quality Commission
CRPD	Convention on the Rights of Persons with Disabilities
DfE	Department of Education
DMD	Duchenne Muscular Dystrophy
DME	Dual and/or Multiple Exceptionalities
DoH	Department of Health
EADSNE	European Agency for the Development of Special Education
EP	Educational Psychologist
EY	Early Years
G&T	Gifted and Talented
GT	Gifted and Talented
HIV	Human immunodeficiency virus
HoC	House of Commons
HPL	High Potential Learning
ICT	Information and communication technology
ITE	Initial Teacher Education
LAC	Looked after Child (by the State)
LD	Learning Difficulties
NAO	National Audit Office
NQT	Newly Qualified Teacher
OECD	Organization for Economic Co-operation and Development
Ofsted	Office for Standards in Education

OHCHR	Office of the High Commissioner for Human Rights
OT	Occupational Therapist
PBIS	Positive Behaviour Interventions and Support
PECs	Picture Exchange Communications System
PhET	Physics Education Technology
PPEO	Policy, Practice (provision), Experiences and Outcomes
Primary School	Equivalent to Elementary School in the USA, covering ages of about five to ten
PRU	Pupil Referral Unit
SALT	Speech and Language Therapist
SAMR	Substitution, Augmentation, Modification and Redefinition
SDG	Sustainable Development Goals
Secondary School	Equivalent to Junior High and High School in USA, covering ages roughly eleven to eighteen years
SETT	Student Environment Tasks Tools
SEMH	Social, emotional and mental health
SEN	Special Educational Needs
SENCo	Special Educational Needs Coordinator
SEND	Special Educational Needs and Disabilities
SLCD	Speech, Language and/or Communication Difficulties
SNA	Special Need Assistant
SpLD	Specific Learning Difficulty
SRP	Specialist Resource Provision
TA	Teaching Assistant
TEACCH	Teaching, Expanding, Appreciating, Collaborating and Cooperating, and Holistic
UD	Universal Design
UDL	Universal Design Learning
UN	United Nations
UNCRC	UN Convention on the Rights of the Child
UNESCO	United Nations Educational, Scientific and Cultural Organization
UNICEF	United Nations International Children's Emergency Fund
VLL	Virtual Learning Lab
VOCA	Voice Output Communication Aid
VR	Virtual reality
WHO	World Health Organization

1

Setting the Context

Daryl Maisey and Verity Campbell-Barr

Case study: Being a penguin

Country: UK

Age group: Mixed

Setting: University

Participants involved: Daryl and one of her students

When discussing experiences of child development Daryl recalled,

> I remember once sitting in a lecture theatre next to a mature student who was employed as an unqualified teacher at the time and was studying to gain her qualified teacher status. As we were listening to the lecturer discuss the methodology of action research, she nudged me, smiled and said, 'who'd have thought that an hour ago I was a penguin!' For me this was one of those defining moments in my career; a moment that I would never forget and one that I would recall time and time again. It was a powerful statement that might have been said in jest but was loaded with meaning. Let me explain. In that statement she captured the very multiplicity of the teacher's role and, as she saw it at the time, the sometimes absurdity of what teachers might do or experience in one day. She had indeed been working with the children in her primary school on project work involving penguins. Over the weeks they had investigated the conservation of penguins, their habitat, their food and their behaviours. They had sung songs, shared stories and written poetry. They had made penguin costumes that culminated in a dressing up fun day for a local community charity. In her recall of events she became animated and disclosed several examples of individualised provision for some of the children in her class who might have struggled with different aspects of the activities experienced. I was struck by her in-depth knowledge of the children and their families, her understanding, her compassion and her ability to adapt to make learning enjoyable for all. And here she was at the end

of a tiring day, engaging in learning about action research methodology and looking forward to finding out more about her chosen focus in order to transform practice. Over the course of our conversation I became aware that she had extensive knowledge and understanding of child development but not in the sense of measuring a child's progress against a set of developmental milestones. She was aware of progress charts and standardised markers, but she used these as indicators and not as definers of children or definers of her practice. Her understanding of child development was shaped by theory, research and experience, through which she had come to know the children and herself.

Introduction

This book is all about coming to know the children that you work with, and yourself. It is a presentation and celebration of shared knowledge and experience from theorists and practitioners from across and beyond the education continuum. It does not present milestones and standardized progress charts to follow, but explores and examines some of the many different elements of a teacher's role that can have a significant impact and/or influence on the development of children and young people. In the chapters, authors have deliberately avoided prescriptive directives and assertions, instead providing informed positions on a number of matters for your consideration. Each chapter has been written in collaboration between teachers, practitioners and lecturers, drawing on theoretical, practical and experiential expertise. The knowledge and experience of those involved provide insights into the complexity of the teacher's role and offer new and experienced teachers' suggestions for enhancing and evolving practice for the benefit of children's learning and development.

Chapter 2 addresses the notion of knowledges and the different ways in which those working with children in educational settings come to 'know' from the theoretical to the experiential. Drawing on sociological perspectives of professional knowledge, the chapter combines this theoretical framing with Julie's journey in becoming a knowledgeable early childhood professional. The focus on early childhood education illustrates that in the book there is a consideration of different 'teachers', who will have undertaken a range of initial and continued professional development journeys in the shaping of their professional self. It is important for us to highlight that we recognize that there are different training trajectories for those who work in education. For example, in early years education the Early Years Initial Teacher Training (EYITT) is a degree-level qualification for those working in the private, voluntary and independent sectors. The EYITT is distinct, for example, to a

BEd: Early Years that comes with Qualified Teacher Status. While in both instances the term 'teacher' is used, the two different training routes have different foci and can lead to different employment trajectories, with varying pay and conditions. The use of the term 'teacher' is not to amalgamate all teachers, with a failure to recognize the subtle differences in how one becomes a teacher, but as shorthand for someone who works with children in an education setting. Thus, throughout the chapters, the term 'teacher' is used with an underlying recognition of the differences in who is a teacher and how they have become a teacher.

Education lenses

To fully appreciate the complexity of education, it is important to recognize that education is entwined with the personal, social, political and economic. Each of these perspectives provides a different lens through which to view education and the role of the teacher, which will have implications for what it is that teachers need to 'know'. As discussed in Chapter 2, everyone has an empirical theory of the world based on their experiences. As such, an individual's experiences of education and teachers will shape what it is that they expect of both. Remember playing 'schools' as a child – did you line the teddies up in front of you, take a register and then guide them through a lesson while they sat obediently, listening and not moving? Although a rather simplistic example, it illustrates how even from a young age we hold assumptions about education, teachers and schools. Further personal experiences will guide you in developing more specific illustrations of education and teachers. For example, memories of outdoor play as a child may ignite a passion for outdoor learning as a teacher (Parker-Rees, 2015). Throughout the book there are opportunities to reflect on your personal empirical theory to consider what it is that you, as a teacher, need to know in support of children's development.

Throughout all of the chapters you will note how the concept of a teacher and what it is that teachers are expected to know is inherently political. Education is the object of policy in many different guises, from curriculums to inspections. However, it is also something of a political tool, often presented in election campaigns as a way in which to right the ills of society. Steven Ball (2008), in his book the *Education Debate*, explores how education is a key political issue, with a continual flow of government initiatives and policies that concern all stages of education. Ball considers how these policies shape not only the nature of education, but also the role of teachers. In his book, Ball highlights how education policy does not occur in a vacuum, but interacts with other areas, such as the use of research evidence to guide the direction of policy – albeit, at times, a selective reading of research evidence. The use of research is frequently on the basis of seeking to find the answer to 'what works', whereby the educating of children is a problem that needs to be fixed. For example, child poverty becomes a problem to be fixed on the basis that it is a cost to society, rather than on a humanist principle that children should not live in poverty (Penn, 2012).

Ball also highlights the economics of education, both in relation to the 'business' of education, whereby education is increasingly delivered based upon a market model of parental choice, but also how education (like other areas of policy) is subject to the impact of austerity. The economic perspective on education is not just in relation to how education is delivered on a structural level or the level of funding that is allocated, the economics of education is also about the economic argument as to why education is important. As touched upon briefly in Chapter 6, the economic argument is premised on human capital theory, whereby investments in education are seen to yield an economic return on children entering adulthood. Human capital represents the knowledge, skills and other attributes that an individual obtains that can then be sold in the employment marketplace for an economic return. In essence, the higher a person's human capital, the higher their economic return. High personal economic returns are good for society as higher wages mean people paying higher taxes, alongside fewer people in unemployment, but also the collective capital of a country helps ensure competitiveness in the global knowledge economy (Campbell-Barr, 2009).

Human capital is framed as developing the economic competitiveness of countries as part of a lifelong learning agenda. Beginning with children in their earliest years, early years education has been positioned as laying the foundation to children's later learning. Each stage of education has been positioned as a means to prepare for the next – early years to primary, primary to secondary and so on. Even on entering adulthood, human capital is premised on notions of personal responsibility and a commitment to one's continued lifelong learning.

The consequence of an economic perspective of education for teachers is that it can have implications for shaping their professional role. Approaches to education, and teaching and learning, become shaped by the 'what works rhetoric' of applying the right techniques at the right times in order to achieve the right outcomes. Not only does this have consequences for the professional practice of a teacher and perceptions of their role, whereby they are frequently positioned as an answer to fixing social ills, but it also has consequences for understandings of the child as a learner, pupil and member of society.

The 'what works' rhetoric has consequences for how the child is constructed, particularly in relation to their development. Debates in early years education serve well in highlighting the way in which policy upholds normative expectations of child development. A mythical normal child, who develops at a prescribed linear rate, acts as a benchmark against which to judge all other children. Those children who do not meet the expectations of the 'normal child' are often labelled as deficient in some way. For example, in early years education children are anticipated to achieve a 'good level of development' in relation to the Early Learning Goals. While there is a well-meaning intention to identify those children who may require additional support, there is also something of a deficit model. Consider the wording of 'good' – is a child who has not met the Early Learning Goals therefore 'bad'? There is also a risk that the failure to achieve 'good' becomes a label that stays with the child throughout their education. An alternative perspective would be to celebrate what children have achieved rather than what they are yet to achieve. While there is inevitably a need to identify children who do require additional support, it is also important not to think that child development is a one-size-fits-all approach. There are commonalities in how children develop, but there are also nuances that reflect the uniqueness of children.

Embedded within political, economical and social discourse are the child and their childhood. Consider for a moment that it is adults that construct notions of childhood and determine the ways in which children are perceived, portrayed, privileged and protected. Consider also how childhood is constantly changing as it is temporal in its reflection of adults in their unique and diverse societies. Childhood is essentially context and time affected. As Smidt (2013, p. 5) explains, childhood is a social construct, 'which means that the idea of what childhood is and what children are like are created by adults', responding to the economic, political, religious and cultural influences of the time. Assuming Smidt's position, as teachers you will have formed ideals of childhood based upon personal biographical histories, knowledge and experiences that are situated within the political, economic and social states of your time. An awareness of your ideals of childhood may reveal some of the underlying values that shape your behaviours in professional practice (Campbell-Barr, 2019). This alertness to influences affecting personal reactions and responses to children and their families is discussed in Chapter 8, where reflection and reflexivity are examined. The chapter explores why teachers may think and behave in the ways they do, and how responses from children and their families may not always be those anticipated or intended, affecting a teacher's resilience. In light of childhood as a social construct and dependent upon context and time, it is perhaps essential that teachers recognize that they cannot know the constructs of childhood formed or experienced by others. What is possible is for teachers to acknowledge that childhood differs for every child. Each child's reality belongs to them in their context and in their time. The constructs of childhood (what it should look like and what it should be) differ for every adult. Each adult's ideal of childhood belongs to them in their context and in their time. Just reflecting upon the difference between your own childhood, your ideal of childhood and the technologically advanced context in which many children are now exposed illustrates difference and diversity that is present and ever changing.

A child entering your educational establishment will be experiencing their unique childhood and this will influence their expectations of you (as their teacher), expectations of whom they might meet, expectations of what they might do, expectations of what they might eat and expectations of how they might be treated (Charlesworth, 2017). They may well be expecting something very different to that devised by you and other adults with influence over what is provided and offered in the educational setting. In preparation and planning for development and learning, a pupil needs to be considered in the context of their childhood influences, including their family, culture and community that are socially, politically and economically situated. In Chapter 7, Johnson and Goodyear present a series of case studies that reveal insights into different relationships that teachers make and their potential influences on pupils' development and learning. The chapter explores how you, as the teacher, should come to know yourself, know your pupils, know your families, know your colleagues, know your professionals and know your collaborative professional communities. There is an emphasis on teachers being tasked with recognizing their own ideals of 'parenthood': acknowledging that judgements might be made without appreciation of the pupils' and their families' unique and diverse lives. It reveals examples where the notion of what might constitute effective parenthood might challenge previously held assumptions and draws attention to expectations that parents might have of teachers. The chapter offers you examples from practice to illustrate how effective relationships can enable pupils a sense of belonging, whilst acknowledging the uniqueness of their childhood and the uniqueness of their families. The chapter concludes with suggestions for how a teacher might ensure that they create the conditions from which respectful 'relational pedagogy' can prosper to enable pupils to learn.

In considering the relationship that teachers make with their children it is equally important to consider how educators listen to children in order to form that relationship. In Chapter 6 Graham and Campbell-Barr explore the concept of listening and the conditions within which this happens. Drawing on experiences of working in early years education, Graham analyses how the notion of listening can often be framed by adult agendas, rather than really considering the perspective of the child. Offering an example from a small-scale research project of taking the time to really listen to a child, Graham highlights how it is more than just listening, but also really hearing the child within the pedagogic relationship. Hearing enables a different relationship to emerge between a child and adult.

Pedagogy is sometimes referred to as *the act* or *the art* of teaching. Essentially, it might be viewed as the approaches teachers take when teaching: the methods and practices adopted by you in the delivery of the curriculum. Pedagogy therefore involves an element of personal preference. As such, theories, research and experiential learning from education and from other disciplines inhabit teachers' choices. Political, social and cultural influences will also manifest in different pedagogical approaches. Some of these might be culturally situated (community expectations) and others might be age and curriculum content dependent. For example, younger pupils may be more actively engaged in learning with concrete materials, whereas older pupils may be learning about the abstract. In either context teachers' pedagogical choices will be informed by what is known about these approaches from theory, research and experience (see Chapter 1). Theories in this context can be understood as ideas that try to explain what might be considered developmentally appropriate for different pupils of different ages. Theories might provide some understanding of how children learn and develop. However, it is important to note that theories and theorists attend to the study of child development and learning from different perspectives and in different contexts. Teachers should be aware that there is criticism of some prevailing and widely referenced theories. These not only question the relevance of the context in which the theory was originally devised, but also suggest that some theories might result in pressures to make all pupils conform to universally presented developmental goals, whilst not acknowledging diversity (Lubeck, 1998). Some theories are presented as linear developments without acknowledgement of potential impact from other factors present and affecting the child. As a cautionary note, theories can support teachers in helping to make sense of teaching and learning, but they should always be critically appreciated within their historical, political and social contexts.

There are different theories that are often referred to in the study of child development such as maturation and developmental theories, including behaviourism. Maturation is typically concerned with the measured growth of children and their physical changes over time. Developmental theories examine behaviour changes that might be directly caused by environmental influences. In Chapter 3, Dowling and Hodson situate their discussions within developmental theory as they examine the impact of health and well-being on pupils' development and the teacher's role. They include discussions relating to nutrition, exercise and environmental factors that are framed within economic and educational policy. They examine how external factors can affect the ways in which children and teachers behave and they offer suggestions for how teachers can look after their own welfare as well as that of their pupils. In addition, throughout the book, chapters refer to behaviourism (Skinner, 1957) where the teacher leads learning (often depicted as the historical and traditional teacher-giving-instruction model); constructivism (Piaget, 1936) where the teacher facilitates learning through experience and largely conducted in isolation; and social constructivism (Vygotsky, 1978) where learning is viewed as a process of collaboration between the teacher and pupil. These simple explanations do not, in any way, depict the complexities of the theories presented but do provide an indication of the theories and theorists that are referred to in sections of this book alongside others such as Bowlby (1958) and Bronfenbrenner (1979). As previously mentioned, these theories are not considered in isolation but seen as complimentary to understanding the child/pupil holistically. Teachers are encouraged to view theories in the context of their pupils' sociological environments, keeping in mind their childhood context and the influence of the family.

The environment

The pedagogic relationship between pupils and teachers is a common theme across the chapters, as examples are presented of how teachers draw on their knowledges of children and child development to inform their professional practice. Embedded in the pedagogic relationship is also the environment – sometimes referred to as the third educator in the pedagogic relationship. Chapter 4 draws attention to the idea of the environment in relation to being outdoors, but it also highlights how the environment is about the resources that are provided within different educational contexts. Drawing on a research project that sought to promote outdoor education, Passy and Gilcrest consider how outdoor education can support a pupil's holistic development. They offer the example of how a school vegetable garden can promote gross and fine motor skills, while also championing healthy eating and supporting a pupil's social and emotional well-being, offering a very overt example of the environment as the third educator.

The role of the environment in the pedagogical relationship can also be about the resources that are provided as aids for children's development. In Chapter 5, Bettany provides some specific examples of different tools that may be provided within a learning environment to support children's understanding of technology. However, the chapter also highlights that in considering the environments that children find themselves in, there is also a need to appreciate that it is a constantly changing environment. The example of technology draws attention to how children's lives are changing as the environment in which they live changes around them. Therefore, in considering the child and their context, it is important to recognize that this is not just about the influence of the family, but also about the wider social environment.

Both Chapters 7 and 9 refer to the ecological model that is most commonly attributed to Bronfenbrenner, although others have sought to develop his work. Our intention is not to go into detail about the ecological model, but to consider how it highlights the dynamic relationship between environmental factors and the child. While the theory is ultimately about understanding how the ecological system impacts on the development of a child, it also provides a visual imagery to consider how the child is embedded within different layers of society – public policy, community, education institutions and their family. The child is not only shaped by these social layers, but they will also shape the social layers. At the core of the ecological model is an appreciation that a child, and their education, does not occur in a vacuum. Teachers need to be mindful of the different layers of the child's environment and how they might be influencing that child's development, but also how the pedagogic environment can then be developed to respond to the needs of the child offering plentiful opportunities to further their development.

The focus of this book is on *Why Do Teachers Need to Know about Child Development?* However, in focusing on you, as teachers, we do not want to forget the children that you will be working with. At the heart of this book, and our interest in editing these chapters, is a genuine awe and amazement in the complexity of child development. Throughout the book there are examples from practice to illustrate how you might engage with the child and their social agency in support of fostering their holistic development. Authors also consider the implications of the examples from practice, and the literature and theory that they are referring to, for educators and their professional roles. Working with children and young people will make you laugh and will make you cry. There are inevitably going to be challenges that you will face and we have revealed some examples of these through the use of case studies and practical examples shared by teachers telling their stories. But ultimately, there is also tremendous reward and great joy – such as being a penguin!

2

The Professional Self

Verity Campbell-Barr and Julie Berry

Introduction

Debates on what is a professional proliferate academic literature, often considering the social role of the profession, the criteria for being a professional, specialized knowledge and who or what determines these features. Explorations of professionalism have been important as they have drawn attention to the power imbalances in the structural identification of who and what is a professional, and how this relates to the perceived social role of a given profession. Such debates on professionalism are important, but it is the notion of 'specialist knowledge' in relation to professionalism that we wish to focus on. Failure to consider what constitutes a professional knowledge-base risks silencing the plentiful and diverse ways that people know how to undertake their professional roles. The focus of this chapter is therefore the knowledgeable professional self, considering both what constitutes professional knowledge and how one comes to know.

In structuring the chapter, we use Julie's journey of becoming a knowledgeable professional in the English early education context. Starting with Julie's experiential knowledge from her time working as a Teaching Assistant, we trace through to her feelings of not knowing and the subsequent development of her theoretical knowledge. We have written around Julie's story through the theoretical framework of the sociology of professional knowledge. The framework provides us with the opportunity to explore the socially integrative function of professional knowledge, whilst warning of anti-intellectual perspectives of professional knowledge that only relies on the experiential in order to consider what and how one knows to work in education.

Julie has worked in early years education, which presents interesting debates around professionalism and the terms used to refer to one's professional role. Early years education represents the services that children access prior to statutory school age, such as nurseries and pre-schools. The early years sector is described as a mixed market economy, whereby private, voluntary, independent (PVI) and maintained (state) services all provide early years education. Where an individual works will influence the qualification that they are required to hold and how their professional role is referred to. For example, those working as teachers in the state sector (such as maintained nursery schools and reception classes) will be required to have a degree and Qualified Teacher Status (QTS). Those working in the PVI sectors do not have to have a degree, and training periods and level of qualification vary depending on the role a person will undertake and where they will work (Georgeson and Payler, 2014). While degree-level qualifications have been introduced for the PVI sectors, firstly as the Early Years Professional Status, and later as Early Years Initial Teacher Training (EYITT), they have prompted considerable debate as to what constitutes a profession and a teacher (Cameron and Millar, 2016). In the chapter we refer to 'teacher' to represent those working in the maintained sector with QTS and early years 'educator' to represent those working in the PVI sectors. We recognize that the use of educator masks that there is no consistency in the initial training of those working in the PVI sectors and the inequalities that exist between the sectors, despite them all working under the Early Years Foundation Stage. We believe these debates are important, but they do little to focus on the importance of professional knowledges, which forms the focus of this chapter.

Window on practice

Julie Berry – Emerging professional knowledge

My professional experience and knowledge that I am drawing from for the purpose of this chapter is from eighteen years of working within the field of education on a full- and part-time basis, alongside undertaking training and entering Higher Education. The aim of my reflective and experiential account is to provide a 'hands on' and 'lived' experience of how I have personally developed within the field. I share my awareness of what I have gained along the way and the impact it has had on my personal and professional self. From reading my story, you may find you can relate to elements of it, or, on the contrary, you may not share in the emotional responses I have encountered when working with young children. Your career progression may also be different, and this is ok as it reflects that there are so many variants within education and so many external and individual influences that impact you along the way. Not one person's journey will be the same. What I do hope to achieve is to leave you with some food for thought about the professional self and instil some ambition (possibly reassurance) that no matter where you are in your career, there is always something to be gained.

My journey began in 2000, I had just completed my A-levels and I was looking for work that related to the psychology qualification I had just achieved.

I successfully gained employment to provide 1:1 support for a child with additional needs and learning difficulties at a local primary school. In summary, my job responsibilities involved providing educational, behavioural and personal support. I made resources, adapted classroom lesson plans so that they were fit for purpose for the child's needs and abilities. I dealt with challenging behaviour and worked alongside many professionals such as teachers, Special Educational Needs Coordinators (SENCos), educational psychologists, speech therapists, teaching assistants and parents.

When taking on this job my experience and knowledge were non-existent, but I strived to be what I thought at the time was child-centred (Bogatić et al., 2018). Over time, my experiential knowledge developed, particularly from working alongside other professionals who modelled aspects of the role, shared resources and offered practical advice. I was fortunate that the teacher whose classroom I was working in provided guidance and appropriate materials for me to take home and read. In-house training also left me with a range of certificates from Safeguarding to Makaton.

I became an active member of the school staff team and as I reflected I could see that my roles involved locus parentis, nurturer, enabler, role model, a voice for the child, behaviourist, educationalist, problem solver, communicator (between home and school), counsellor and family worker. I was also an administrator (I actually enjoyed the paperwork) and an expert in policy-related tasks, such as Individual Education Plans, risk assessments, reports for speech therapists, referral forms and assessment frameworks – to name a few!!

The social and the professional self

Julie's introduction to her professional journey in education begins to illustrate a number of points that are important when considering the professional-self, particularly in relation to professional knowledges and skills. Julie's account of the early stages of her professional career illustrates that the professional-'self' is not individual, nor isolated from other professions. Professionalism is related to the social construction of the profession and its social function. For example, a 'teacher' implies someone who teaches. What they teach (and how) will be determined by the social expectations of the profession – what it is that society believes teachers should/can 'do' and the outcomes that are desired of that profession. The expectations will be specific to the time and place in which the teacher is located. For example, what is required of a teacher today in England is different to 200 years ago, as well as being different to a teacher in Chile or Ukraine. Whilst there might be shared, common attributes to the role of a teacher, the social construction of the profession means that it is highly influenced by the social-historic context. Embedded in this context will be a whole host of influences, including political and economic ones that will inform the social function of the profession.

Understanding the role of a particular profession is often related to other professions. Pertinent to this chapter is the distinction between 'teacher' and 'educator' that we established earlier. Defining a teacher in the English context is increasingly complex due to changes in government policy around the management of schools and who can be employed as a teacher (see Furlong and Whitty, 2017), but our arguments resonate across the sectors. The distinction between teachers and educators reflects the English context in which Julie worked, but is not unique to it. In many countries, there are different training requirements for those going on to work with children of different ages, often in response to both the perceived needs of the children and related constructions of the purpose of the professionals working with those children (Oberhuemer, Schreyer and Neuman, 2010). For example, within the early years, there has been a historic divide between 'care' and 'education', whereby younger children were identified as needing substitute care whilst their parents worked and older children required education in preparation for school (Campbell-Barr, 2019a; Moss, 2006). However, the 'education' focus within the early years has been identified as distinct and different to that of a teacher in a primary school, symbolic in the use of a term such as pre-school. Consequently, there is a perception that those working in the early years perform a different social purpose to those working in schools and, accordingly, require different knowledges and skills.

International examples illustrate the distinction in professional roles between teachers and early years professionals. In many European countries, the term 'pedagogue' is adopted to refer to those working in early years. However, Anglo-American terminology struggles with the use of the term 'pedagogue' (Jensen, 2016), often translating it as 'teacher', but this is seen as inappropriate within the context of early years. The term 'teacher' does not account for how the term 'pedagogue' has a much broader interpretation than that of a person who teaches. Instead, the term 'pedagogue' has a more holistic interpretation that encompasses care, education and upbringing (Moss, 2006). Therefore, increasingly 'educator' is adopted in translations to make a distinction between what is regarded as formal teaching in schools and the more holistic approach to children's development found in early years education (Campbell-Barr, 2019a).

The distinction between teacher and educator reflects that there are different social functions for the two roles. Establishing the role and purpose of a profession is important as it has a bearing on what are the knowledges and skills that are required of that profession. As Julie's account has already illustrated, there are many performative and technocratic aspects to a profession, such as the paperwork that she referred to. Technocratic professionalism implies there are set techniques within a profession to achieve the desired outcomes. The completing of paperwork is a simplistic example, as the wider implication of technocratic professionalism is that if a society wants a profession to achieve X, the knowledges and skills required will therefore be those that enable X to be reached. However, anyone who has ever worked with children will tell you that there is no such easy formula of applying the right knowledges and skills at the right times in order to achieve the desired outcomes.

Looking at Julie's introduction, it is possible to identify that the knowledges and skills she required were both multiple and varied. The description of her multiple roles – *nurturer, enabler, role model, a voice for the child, etc.* – illustrate the knowledges required, whilst the discussion of her exams and experiential knowledge begin to illustrate the different ways in which a person comes to obtain knowledge.

Reflective questions

1. Where do you obtain the knowledge and skills to undertake your professional role?
2. Is there a clear distinction between experiential knowledge and other forms of coming to know?

Sociology of professional knowledge

The sociology of professional knowledge provides a framework with which to consider both the multiple forms of knowledge for working within education and the different ways in which a person comes to know. The emphasis on knowledges (knowledge in the plural) is intentional, as throughout this chapter we want to emphasize the complexities and multiplicities of professional knowledges when working in education.

Considering professional knowledges inevitably raises the question as to what is knowledge – something of a perpetual debate that has been considered from a range of different perspectives. Theoretical considerations of knowledge are often arbitrarily divided between those positioned as scientific and those that are philosophical. Whilst the divide is a broad one, it begins to illustrate that there are different perspectives as to what 'knowledge' is, how that knowledge is determined and how it is validated (Furlong and Whitty, 2017). However, rather than an arbitrary split between scientific and philosophical knowledge, we want to explore how professional knowledges come in different forms, with different processes for determining and validating it.

There are various methods for determining what knowledge is, which will be tied to the traditions of different disciplines (and related professions). The different forms of knowledge and their processes for determining and validating knowledge are well illustrated with the work of Bernstein. Bernstein's (Bernstein, 1999; Bernstein, 2000) work can be a little impenetrable at times, so it is helpful to draw on those who have sought to further explore his ideas (Hordern, 2017; Young, 2007; Young and Muller, 2007). Bernstein (1999) distinguished between different forms of knowledge and their different structures and social conditions through which the knowledge is determined and validated. A simple overview of his knowledges is as follows:

> Vertical discourse, hierarchical structured A structured, coherent form of knowledge that enables it to be distributed, tested and challenged and related to other forms of knowledge and history (Young and Muller, 2007).
> Vertical discourse, horizontally structured: Some degree of a common core, but with different languages, perspectives and processes for testing and validating the knowledge.
> Horizontal discourse: Local, context-dependent everyday knowledge.

The names of the different forms of knowledge are perhaps a little confusing, but they seek to illustrate that there are different forms of knowledge – from the highly structured to the everyday. The structure is important as it determines the different ways in which the forms of knowledge are socially validated. Firstly, vertical discourse with a hierarchical structure is exemplified by a discipline such as maths, whereby knowledge can be scientifically verified through logical and/or set mathematical procedures. There are clear, agreed and shared processes within the discipline to determine and validate knowledge. Epistemological hierarchies have seen an emphasis on vertical discourse with a hierarchal structure as positivistic approaches to determining and validating knowledge have been privileged for their structure, rigour and assumed objectivity.

To illustrate vertical discourse with a horizontal structure, Bernstein used the example of sociology, a discipline that has various strands that have varying processes for sharing, testing and validating knowledge. As such, there is the common core of sociology, but its various fractions have different approaches for testing and validating knowledge. The different processes for determining and validating knowledge are localized to the specific strand. Thus, whilst there is a shared understanding within a specific strand/discipline, the different strands do not necessarily have shared understandings and/or meaning. Lastly, horizontal knowledge represents the everyday knowledge that individuals develop through their experiences, such as knowledge of the daily routine of a school.

Relating these different knowledge structures to Julie's professional knowledge, it is possible to see signs of her knowledges from the theoretical to the everyday. Each form of knowledge has a social process for its validation, from those of the (socially) agreed approaches for testing and verifying knowledge evident in the vertical discourse to those of the (social) relevance of everyday knowledge. It is not uncommon for professionals to focus on the everyday knowledge as its experiential nature provides both a closeness and relevance to it. In essence, I have experienced it, so I know it to be true. Conversely, vertical discourse can feel dislocated from the knower (Bernstein, 2000), being constructed at a distance to the profession, often at a point in history that the professional is not connected to. However, it is important to recognize that experience alone does not constitute knowing and this is evident in the questions that were arising for Julie.

Window on practice

Julie Berry – Evolving professional knowledge

I was approached by the head teacher to become a qualified teacher. I loved being a Teaching Assistant, the experiences I was gaining, the relationships I had developed with the children, staff and parents were important to me, so I felt torn as to whether completing my Bachelor of Education was the right career choice for me. It would have been the answer to my lack of curriculum awareness, theory of child development and background information on the movement from special schools to mainstream inclusion, funding constraints, etc. However, from the experience I had gained my interests were leaning more towards a holistic role in 'early intervention' rather than a role within an education setting.

To pursue my interest in early intervention, I took a job at a local pre-school as a play assistant. Although I loved the day-to-day work, I was in need of some qualification support. The manager accepted my request to undertake an NVQ3 in Childcare and Development. It entailed a series of modules and a first aid course. Modules consisted of building positive relationships and communication; developing and maintaining healthy environments for children; safeguarding; and promoting healthy development, to name a few. For me, the qualification consolidated my experiential knowledge and what I knew from the setting's policies, such as whistle blowing, safeguarding, the managerial structure of my setting and roles and responsibilities of each person within the setting. I was observed preparing children for going out in the garden on a summers' day (putting on hats, sun cream, providing areas of shade, access to drinks, etc.), and I was observed carrying out our rhyme time, which involved singing and action songs. I successfully gained the qualification and continued working at the setting.

Over time I took on a play leader role to provide services to vulnerable children and families within the community and in hard-to-reach areas. I began learning about the community I lived in, their difficulties and the impact that living in deprivation could have on children's learning and development. I encountered the struggles young single mums were experiencing when assessing what support we could provide parents and children. I was appointed to run sessions such as treasure baskets for babies, young family support groups and single parent groups. All involved a multi-professional approach with Citizen Advice sessions available, drugs and alcohol support, and the Job Centre visiting once a month to support those on benefits and those that may be entitled to additional support.

My role was fast paced, so I was drawing on all my previous experiences to date and the ongoing in-house training I was receiving. There was always a new agenda, a new initiative, a new job title and new approaches to professional practice. I was drawing on all of my experiences, alongside what had been modelled to me and explained on training courses, to enhance my professional standards. However, I felt I was a passive recipient of a managerial discourse and I needed more knowledge to develop my professional self. I wanted to know the theory, origin, political reasons behind all the change and how it benefitted me in my role. Most importantly, I wanted to know how best to support the children and families I was working with daily. I wanted to validate my experiential knowledge and expand it. I reduced my working hours to casual staff and embarked on a full-time BA (Hons) Early Childhood Studies degree with the University of Plymouth.

Building on experience

The experiential knowledge that Julie developed during her professional working roles can be related to the horizontal discourse of Bernstein's knowledges discussed earlier. Whilst horizontal knowledge was discussed earlier in relation to workplace practice, everyone will have an empirical theory of the world based on their experiences (Winch, 2014). People know a lot about the world around them from being a part of the culture (Johnson, 2000). For example, most people (particularly in Western cultures) will have attended school, maybe even pre-school, and this will provide them with an understanding of what a school is like, what happens there and what the professionals 'do' whilst there. For those who work in educational contexts, there will be additional layers to this knowledge, as the professional self will have experienced things such as the challenges that Julie identified in relation to bureaucracy, working with families and getting to know about those families with additional challenges. However, her dissatisfaction with her professional knowledges signals that experience alone is not enough to know how to work in an educational context.

Recognizing that experience alone is not enough to constitute a knowledgeable professional self is important for a number of reasons. Firstly, beyond the assumption that someone would be their most knowledgeable on the day they retire if they only needed experience in order to 'know', relying on experiential knowledge also implies that all knowledge is out there waiting to be experienced, but not all forms of knowledge are experienced. Furthermore, the focus on experience risks an individualistic approach to knowledge as there is no scalability to the knowledge

(Biesta, 2014) – just because I have experienced it and know it to be true, does that mean others have? New knowledge (or new experiences) has no relationship to history or the wider context, risking a de-intellectualizing of the professional self (Young and Muller, 2014).

Education as a discipline should, at this point, be established as different to teacher/educator training and education. A discussion of education as a discipline would present a different argument on knowledges to that of exploring the professional self, as professional knowledge in teaching may not be the same as knowledge in the study of education (Furlong and Whitty, 2017). Within professional knowledge, the balance between different forms of knowledge will vary depending on perspectives of how to combine them, concepts of teaching, education and the profession. Often combinations of knowledge are presented as a balance between theory and practice. However, this balance has been variable throughout history as well as internationally. In England, there have been criticisms of too much theory or theory being imposed, and successive governments have adjusted the educating of teachers accordingly in seeking to find a 'solution' to the problem. However, often the offer of solutions fails to acknowledge the complexities of the coming together of knowledges and skills for informing professional practice.

To find a solution, a problem must first be identified. Arguably, in England, the historical evolution of teacher education has seen an increasing move towards competence-based models. Competence models (at least within the English language) imply a list of attributes against which an individual can be judged. There is an implied simplicity of identifying the 'right' competences to achieve the desired outcomes, failing to consider a more holistic interpretation of professional knowledge (Urban et al., 2011). Competence models also fail to identify with the place of knowledges, with an emphasis on skills due to a 'what works' approach to professional practice. A person can exercise a skill, but without necessarily understanding the reasoning behind the skill – just as Julie identified on her professional journey.

Recognition that experience alone is not enough in the development of the professional self is well illustrated when considering training models for education professionals, whereby there is a combination of theory and practice. Internationally, degree courses for those going on to work in teaching or as educators have a combination of taught theoretical content alongside time in placement (also referred to as practicum). The time in practice recognizes the importance of experiential knowledge, whilst the theory provides the connection to history and context, enabling an individual to relate their emerging knowledges generated through experience to the history of knowledges that has gone before. In particular, in returning to Bernstein's vertical discourse (of both kinds), the history enables a connection to how the knowledges developed and their history of being tested and validated. This historical knowledge-bank provides professionals with a rich array of resources to draw upon to develop their professional practice.

Window on practice

Julie Berry – Professional confidence

From my very first lecture, through to my last, I knew I had made the right choice. It was everything I imagined and more. I learnt about the importance of play, working with colleagues, child development theories, learning theories, brain development, concepts of childhood throughout history and the impact they have on services, job roles and children's lives. I learnt about research methods, how to critique and analyse topics I was coming across, such as gender development, current issues within the profession, children and the power of media, outside provision, whether inclusion is exclusion for SEN children, etc. The lecturers provided international, historical and multi-disciplinary perspectives through drawing on their wealth of experience bringing the acquisition of knowledge and pedagogy to life.

One module required a placement, whilst promoting reflective practice. It allowed me to relate my job roles to what I was learning at university. This was a valuable time as I was able to take all of the theory I had learnt in lectures, read about in books and analysed in essays and consolidate it to provide new meaning to my practice. This gave me a real grounding on my own beliefs and developed my confidence within my role as I knew why I was working the way I was.

A multi-disciplinary profession

Julie's time undertaking the BA in Early Childhood Studies not only enabled her to forge links between theory and practice, but also illustrates the multi-disciplinary nature of learning to work with children. The multi-disciplinarity is pertinent to any professional role within education, but is well illustrated by Early Childhood Studies. Julie's account of her degree identifies how it is one that draws upon psychology, sociology, biology, neuro-science, social policy, cultural studies and more. Rhedding-Jones (2005) discusses that the early years is a theoretical hybrid, whereby there is no one discipline that can be identified as its core. While developmental psychology might be identified as the roots to the theoretical origins of Early Childhood Studies, socio-cultural theories and sociology have more recently influenced its theoretical understandings. However, it is not just that Early Childhood Studies is theoretically diverse, but also that the different disciplines represent Bernstein's vertical discourse, horizontally structured. As such, there is no single discipline, but also within those disciplines, no single way for identifying, describing, testing and validating knowledge.

Internationally, early years educators are recognized as a profession that is multi-disciplinary (Campbell-Barr, 2019a). Inevitably, there are variations to the extent with which different countries draw upon the varying disciplines, but ultimately those undertaking initial training to work as early years educators and teachers will be studying a range of disciplines. Furthermore, to add to the complexities, those disciplines might not harmoniously fit together, and there can be criticisms within the different disciplines. For example, historical theories on developmental psychology have been criticized for a presumed linear approach to child development, whereby socio-cultural perspectives have challenged developmentalism, highlighting the influence of social factors on children's development. In considering the influence of social factors we refer back to Bernstein's use of sociology as an illustrative example of vertical knowledge, horizontally structured, whereby there is the discipline of sociology, but various sub-disciplines embedded within it, each of which has a perspective on the influence of society on one's development.

Window on international research

Urban, M., Vandenbroek, M., Lazzari, A., Peeters, J. and van Laere, K. (2011) Competence Requirements in Early Childhood Education and Care (CoRe), London and Ghent: University of East London, University of Ghent and European Commission Directorate-General for Education and Culture. Available at: https://download.ei-ie.org/Docs/WebDepot/CoReResearchDocuments2011.pdf.

The 'study on competence requirements in early childhood education and care' (CoRe) undertook an international literature review, a survey to explore competence profiles in fifteen European countries and case studies of interesting practice in seven European countries (Urban et al., 2011, p. 13) to explore the competence requirements of those working in early childhood education and care (ECEC). The study identified the centrality of competence requirements of the workforce to the quality of ECEC services, but that there are multiple pathways towards professional development. Therefore, competence requirements should not be seen as prescriptive, but as part of a competence system. The study concluded that the ECEC workforce is more than just the sum of the competences of individuals, but a complex interaction between the individuals' competences and the repeated occurrence of theory and practice.

There is a risk that the professional knowledge-base for teachers and early years educators is seen as unstable as a result of its variety and the varying criticisms. For those becoming teachers and early years educators, the multi-disciplinarity of the professions and the criticisms that exist within and between the disciplines can result in a sense of confusion. Rather than contributing to a sense of knowing, professionals will question which form of knowledge is most persuasive and will best guide their professional practice. The answer to such questions relates to both a professional's epistemological assumptions and the coming together of knowledges, whereby the multi-disciplinarity provides opportunities for the professional self.

A professional's epistemological perspective represents their beliefs as to what constitutes knowledge and how individuals 'know'. Most people will have a view of how the world is based on their participation in it (Winch, 2004). One's epistemological perspective provides a holistic view as to how knowledge is viewed and our relationship to that knowledge. An individual's epistemological perspective will determine what they think is true, whereby they will favour some disciplines over others because the discipline reflects their epistemological stance.

Earlier, we discussed that vertical knowledge in its two forms – hierarchical and horizontal – has different processes for establishing, sharing, testing and validating knowledge. Epistemological hierarchies favour hierarchical structures, as the 'testing' of knowledge, through agreed, reliable and valid approaches, is regarded as providing a rigour to the knowledge. The rigour offers social facts and an agreed way of knowing the world. However, the influence of different disciplines in the early years illustrates that hierarchical knowledge is not always seen as being able to provide all the answers. For some, the horizontal structure will illustrate that there are multiple realities. While this is a very broad (and crude) distinction of ways of knowing, it illustrates how there are different perspectives as to what constitutes knowledge and that individuals can also hold different perspectives. Where for one professional things can only be true if there is hard reliable evidence, for another there is no single truth. These perspectives will influence which disciplines professionals identify with, whereby the processes of establishing and verifying knowledge will help persuade an individual of its usefulness. For example, some professionals will be swayed by neuro-science, others post-structuralism.

While individuals will favour some knowledge over others, there is no need to single out one form of knowledge for meeting the demands of professional practice. In fact, the demands of professional practice will require multiple forms of knowledge. Firstly, the multi-disciplinarity of teacher and early years educator professionalism enables individuals to draw on different forms of knowledge to meet the demands of professional practice. This provides a richness to professional practice as professionals are able to form knowledge combinations to meet the demands of the context in which they work.

Importantly, the knowledge combinations face two ways, one to theory (vertical discourses) and one to practice (horizontal discourse). As such, professionals will draw upon the theory that they know, in combination with the knowledge that they have developed through experience to meet the demands of the context (Campbell-Barr, 2019b). Meeting the demands of the context is not a linear process of taking knowledge X and Y and applying them in practice. Instead, professionals will be balancing different forms of knowledge, combining them to varying extents, possibly never forming the same knowledge combinations on more than one occasion.

Professionals will learn about how different forms of knowledge can come together and which forms of knowledge are negotiable and which are not. Non-negotiable knowledge is not necessarily vertical, hierarchically structured knowledge. Horizontal (everyday) knowledge, which can include the daily routines, habits and cultures of early years settings and schools, may also be non-negotiable. Other forms of non-negotiable knowledge may be those that relate to national standards or the expectations of parents (for example) and this can generate points of tension.

The change in knowledge combinations will not only relate to the subtleties of the changes that occur in professional practice, but also to how professionals will evaluate the knowledge combinations and their usefulness. For example, the knowledges applied to meet the demands of listening to a two-year-old who is reluctant to share (see Chapter 6) will vary between each two year old, as well as changing as the two year old changes. Professionals will also evaluate the effectiveness of the knowledges – in simple terms they will reflect on what went well (potentially reproducing it at a future point in time) and what they would change and do differently. Not only does this mean that the process of coming to know is ongoing, but also that the knowledge developed in everyday practice (horizontal knowledge) has the potential to influence theory. This is well illustrated when considering the work of early years pioneers such as the McMillan sisters or Montessori, whereby their observations of everyday practice now shape theoretical knowledge in the early years (Nutbrown and Clough, 2014).

However, we would add a note of caution to our outline of how knowledges combine to inform professional practice and the importance of reflecting on these combinations – focusing solely on the professional self risks knowledge being individualized and lacking in scale. Therefore, an important part of developing professional knowledges is ensuring they are shared and distributed. The sharing and distributing of knowledge enable them to be tried out by others. It is this 'trying out' that supports the process of testing and validating different forms of knowledge. Stating something to be true or known may just be an individual experience of truth (Biesta, 2014); thus, sharing supports the process of validating the knowledge on a larger scale.

Conclusion

To talk of theoretical and practical knowledge as forming the basis of professional knowledge perpetuates a divide between the two, obscuring the relationship between them and an investigation of what the balance between them looks like (Young and Muller, 2014). Instead, in viewing professional knowledge as looking two ways – to theory and practice – it provides a richness to the professional knowledge-base.

Furthermore, for teachers and early years educators, the theoretical knowledge-base is rich and diverse, drawing on a range of disciplines that provides opportunities for professionals to form different knowledge combinations to meet the demands of their practice. Coming to know as a professional is complex as a result of the range of knowledges that exist. Becoming a professional is also an ongoing process, as professionals experiment with different knowledge combinations, but it is also ultimately an enriching and rewarding process.

Reflective questions

As a professional how do you engage with the core themes of this chapter:

1. that knowledge comes in different forms;
2. that being an educator or teacher is multi-disciplinary; and
3. the combination of practical and theoretical knowledge.

Reflexive question

As a professional how do you engage with these core themes in relation to your own emotions and assumptions and biases?

Annotated bibliography

Campbell-Barr, V. (2019b). 'Professional knowledges for early childhood education and care', *Journal of Childhood Studies*, 44(1), pp. 134–46.
This paper explores the different ways in which knowledge can be conceptualized when considering professional practice in early childhood education and care. In particular, the paper considers phronesis (practical wisdom) as a form of knowledge that guides the work of early childhood professionals.

Hordern, J. (2017). 'Bernstein's sociology of knowledge and education(al) studies', in Furlong, J. and Whitty, G. (eds.) *Knowledge and the study of education: An international exploration*. Oxford: Symposium Books.
In this chapter Hordern explains Bernstein's sociological perspectives of knowledge in an accessible style. The chapter explores the contribution of Bernstein to notions of professionalism and understandings of professional practice.

3

The Need for Health and Well-Being

Maria Dowling and Mary Hodson

Introduction

Teachers and other professionals working within schools and other educational settings regularly encounter situations in which health and well-being can be seen to impact directly or indirectly not only on the holistic development of children and young people, but also on the professionals themselves. With this in mind, consider the following:

1. Can you think of a particular child whose development and academic achievement were affected by health and well-being issues? What was the nature of the issues and how did they impact on the child within the school/ setting?
2. Does your school/setting have a policy on health and well-being in relation to children and young people? Are there other policies within the setting, which relate to children/young people's physical and emotional health?
3. How are the health and well-being needs of staff supported? Consider formal and informal systems within your organization including those available through your Human Resources department, if applicable.
4. How do you support your own health and well-being? What strategies do you have in place to ensure that you maintain optimum physical and emotional health?
5. Why is there a growing recognition of the importance of health and well-being in schools and other educational settings? Why do teachers need to know about health and well-being and the implications for child development?

In this chapter, the notions of health and well-being are explored and discussed in relation to the holistic development of children and young people and also in relation to the teachers who work with them. Health and well-being are considered within the wider context of economic and educational policy that directly influences and impacts upon the physical and emotional day-to-day lives of pupils and their teachers. The chapter explores why teachers, particularly those in the early stages of their careers, need to know and understand the significance of health and well-being and how they might seek the support of others to ensure that they address the welfare needs of not only their pupils but also their own.

The importance of health and well-being has been well documented of late – barely a week goes by without some aspect of this broad topic being brought to our attention within the press or on social media. The role of health and well-being within education is certainly more prominent today than it was fifty years ago and sometimes, for some professionals working within education, it can appear that there is no end to the increasing expectations placed upon education staff, including teachers, head teachers and education support staff in relation to pupils' health and well-being (Jourdan, 2011). Whilst this focus on health and well-being may be seen by some as a diversion from the core business of educating children (Ofsted, 2018), and another responsibility or element that educators must fit into an increasingly busy schedule, it also highlights the pivotal role and privileged access that teachers have in relation to the lives of children, families and communities in Western society today. Whilst it is recognized that teachers may not be specialists in physical or mental health, nevertheless in the UK, the Children Act 2004 emphasized the expectation that teachers are one of a number of professionals who hold collective responsibility for the welfare of children. Teachers work within a legal framework, which is designed to protect and support the development of children and young people. Legislation and practice guidance reflect both the rights of children and the rights of staff in relation to health and well-being, and the sometimes contradictory messages that emanate from these must be translated into school/setting policy and implemented in practice.

The importance of providing opportunities for children and young people to experience and manage challenge is well documented (Bento and Dias, 2017; DfE, 2014a; DfE, 2017b; Waite et al., 2016). However, such opportunities may well involve some element of risk, whether this is in the outdoor learning environment or within the classroom. These opportunities need to be carefully risk-assessed within the context of Health and Safety legislation and regulation (Health and Safety at Work Act, 1974, The Management of Health and Safety Regulations, 1999). School and setting policies and procedures interpret these complex legislative and regulatory texts for their unique contexts, taking into account the developmental needs of the pupils attending. Differing knowledge and experience is likely to result in head teachers and managers of settings having different perspectives in terms of what constitutes appropriate risk, and this ultimately impacts upon the available opportunities for pupils and staff. Off-site activities such as school trips or access to a paddling pool for young children attending early years' provision may be considered too risky to undertake by some head teachers or managers, whilst in other similar organizations such activities may be offered whilst ensuring that risk of any harm is minimized. The underlying issue here is supporting teachers to recognize and understand the difference between 'risk', as an essential element of new learning 'where there is uncertainty about the outcomes' (Tovey, 2007, p. 100), and the notion of 'hazard' which implies an element of harm is present.

There may be occasions where understandings of risk may differ and the views of teachers may conflict with the views of other teachers, head teachers or managers in relation to the appropriateness of learning activities. However, teachers need to be alert to evidence that suggests the elimination of risk in learning, as defined by Tovey (2007), 'can hinder independence and development' particularly in young children (Nikiforidou, 2017, p. 620). Accepting that risk is present in new learning enables teachers to begin to consider ways in which pupils might have space to try out new skills and present new ideas, with confidence. The challenge for teachers is that risk is referred to in practices and documentation that indicates potential harm, and this can be where confusion arises. For example, there are occasions where teachers are asked to undertake 'risk' assessments. These are often associated with planned activities where an element of harm may be suggested. As teachers, you need to be clear whether you are assessing an appropriate level of risk in learning (where the outcome is unknown) and hazard, where pupils may be exposed to harm. Risk assessment is primarily a matter of judgement, which may be influenced by individual knowledge, experience and professional opinion. Undertaking risk assessment should therefore include consideration of the skills and experience of the staff involved. For example, a newly qualified teacher may require more support than an experienced member of staff and teachers should not be asked to undertake an activity with which they are uncomfortable. Policies and procedures must take account of the needs of pupils and staff. Adherence to school policy and procedure should guide staff – always check with your line manager if you are unsure.

Reflective questions

1. What do you consider is meant by risk in a learning context?
2. How do you define the difference between risk and hazard?

Reflexive questions

1. What is influencing your interpretations of 'risk'?
2. What has shaped your understanding and behaviours in relation to 'risk' to date?

Discussions with a number of experienced practitioners as preparation for writing this chapter, in addition to our own experience as teachers, suggest that the capacity of children to grow, develop and learn is intrinsically linked to their health and well-being (Public Health England, 2014) – in this sense, the health and well-being of pupils are certainly the business of educators. Internationally, it is also widely recognized that a child's health and well-being impact upon their cognitive development and capacity to learn (Jukes, Drake and Bundy, 2007). This view has been well supported by literature (Blossner, 2009). Promoting children's health and well-being in schools does not mean that teachers should substitute teaching for healthcare duties – rather, it requires teachers to work effectively within an institutional context that enables them to fully carry out their educational tasks. This reality is reflected in a number of policy initiatives and embodied in the Teachers' Standards (DfE, 2011; DfE, 2013a).

Definitions

There is currently no consensus on a definition of health and well-being. The biomedical model as exemplified by the functionalist perspective of Parsons (1951) focuses exclusively on physical and biological factors, and does not take into consideration the many psychological, environmental and social influences on an individual's or community's health. However, the World Health Organization (WHO) (2019) adopts a more holistic perspective that considers health to be based upon the interaction between the individual and their environment, which may include social, cultural, environmental and economic factors. This holistic approach emphasizes the intrinsic relationship between mind, body and spirit and is reflected in the WHO Constitution, which defines health in its broadest sense as 'a state of complete physical, mental and social wellbeing and not merely the absence of disease or infirmity' (WHO, 2019, webpage). Whilst some may argue that the biomedical model remains prevalent within modern medicine, the influence of the WHO (which functions as part of the United Nations to focus on global health issues) can be seen within a range of education policies and initiatives highlighting the importance of physical and emotional health to support children's holistic development.

In addition to the focus on physical health and the potential impact of disability on learning (Department for Education and Department for Health, 2015), the importance of mental health has increasingly been highlighted as an issue within society in recent years. This has been reflected in the WHO strengthening their position in relation to mental health and highlighting their view of mental health as 'an integral and essential' component of overall health. In referring back to their definition of health, the WHO recognize that an important implication of mental health is

more than just the absence of mental disorders or disabilities. Mental health is a state of well-being in which an individual realizes his or her own abilities, can cope with the normal stresses of life, can work productively and is able to make a contribution to his or her community.

(WHO, 2018b, webpage)

The influence of the WHO can be seen to be extensive and influential in underpinning welfare and educational initiatives around the world.

The Teachers' Standards relating to practice in England (DfE, 2011, p. 10) make it very clear that the education of pupils is a teacher's primary concern and that they 'are accountable for achieving the highest possible standards in work and conduct'. However, although it is implicit in Standard 5, the Standards make no explicit mention of the importance of a teacher's or pupil's well-being, or of its impact on a teacher's ability to teach, or a pupil's ability to learn. Nevertheless, teachers are required to do all that they can to protect the health, safety and well-being of the pupils in their care. This legal responsibility originates from three separate sources:

1. The common law duty of care – that has arisen out of past cases and customs, rather than statutes.
2. The statutory duty of care – such as the Children Act 1989 or Working Together to Safeguard Children (2018).
3. The teacher's contract of employment.

Alongside their duty of care, it could be argued that in order to meet the requirement to protect pupils' well-being, teachers have a duty of care to themselves too. There is a growing body of evidence, which suggests that a teacher's well-being has a positive impact on successful student outcomes (Paterson and Grantham, 2016; Wang and Zuccollo, 2020). A report by Education Support Partnership (2017) (a UK-based charity offering well-being and mental health support services to educationalists) identified that 36 per cent of teachers whose own well-being had been compromised felt that it had a negative impact on their pupils' studies and 13 per cent felt it had a negative impact on their results. Therefore, due consideration should be given to factors which can impact both pupils' and teachers' well-being. There are a number of these that might threaten well-being, including (but not limited to) nutrition, obesity and being overweight, exercise, environment and an increase in mental health issues. The following sections explore each of these in turn, using case studies to illustrate some of the influences present in practice situations from around the world.

Nutrition

It is estimated that 3 million pupils in the UK are at risk of going hungry during school holidays (Forsey, 2017), and it is reported that their food preferences, food choices and eating behaviours are influenced by their parents (Kyttälä et al., 2014).

However, primary school-aged pupils spend six and a half hours or more a day (in term time) at school, which encompasses at least one mealtime. Therefore, it is possible for schools (and teachers) to influence their food habits. In the United States, a programme of eight one-hour lessons, which included hands on food preparation, was delivered by teachers to 367 pupils aged seven to fourteen years in schools in Miami and Chicago. The programme was found to have increased pupils' nutrition knowledge, vegetable intake and healthy behaviours. This indicated nutrition education as important (Roth et al., 2017) demonstrating that teachers can be influential in shaping pupils' behaviours and knowledge around food. Hall, Chai and Albrecht (2017) acknowledge that teachers should be involved throughout the planning and assessment of any classroom-based nutrition education intervention being devised by nutrition experts to address teachers' perspectives and facilitate successful delivery. A study by Vio et al. (2018) identified that teachers in fifth grade in Chile (Year 6 in England) not only demonstrated poor eating habits but cited lack of time, money and will to improve as barriers to change. Given how they can influence pupils' behaviours, teachers should model healthy attitudes to food, not only for their pupils' sake, but because eating well also positively impacts upon their own well-being.

Tips for teachers

Eat breakfast: pupils cannot learn on an empty stomach, nor can you teach on one. Keeping simple healthy foods available, like fruit, yogurt, granola or whole-wheat cereal, is essential. Plus, they are filling and nutritious.

Keep healthy snacks to hand: for days when you might be hungrier than usual or need a boost. Some schools have 'Friday Treats' in the staff area/room. Why not offer healthy options, such as vegetables or fruit, if you can contribute?

Stay hydrated: keep water (bottle or cup) near you so you can take fluids whenever you need to. Try to limit how much tea or coffee you drink, especially if you like it loaded with sugar, and definitely steer clear of fizzy drinks: they are a waste of calories (and not what you want to model to the pupils in your care).

Reflective question

How do you influence the nutritional behaviours of pupils?

Reflexive questions

1. How did you feel in response to the above section that implies that you, as the teacher, 'should model healthy attitudes to food'?
2. Why do you think you felt that way?
3. What is influencing your responses?

Case Study A: The importance of healthy nutrition

Country: Australia

Age group: Ten to eleven years old

Setting: Mainstream primary school

Participants involved: Pupil A, an eleven-year-old boy and his class teacher

Pupil A was attending school regularly (although frequently late for registration). Some mornings he was disruptive in class, verbally or even physically aggressive towards other children and unable to concentrate in lessons. The class teacher wondered whether this behaviour might be related to Pupil A's home situation: one of his parents had recently been diagnosed with cancer and undergone treatment, but on enquiry it transpired that the parent was in remission and that, if anything, home life had settled. It then emerged that Pupil A was not eating breakfast at home before coming to school.

Outcomes Once a plan was implemented to ensure that he had some nourishment in the mornings, Pupil A's behaviour, mood and attitude to learning improved.

What we can learn Teachers need to be mindful of what is happening to the pupil outside of the classroom/school/setting. They must be aware of factors influencing the pupil. They need to put the pupil at the centre of everything they do and understand how a pupil's systems impact upon one another (Bronfenbrenner, 1992).

Obesity and being overweight

In recent years, it has become more widely recognized that childhood obesity is not just a medical issue but is complex, socially and psychologically (Harrist et al., 2017). Nevertheless, obesity and being overweight have significant health implications for children and adults alike, including being at greater risk of developing type 2 diabetes, asthma, hypertension (high blood pressure), cancer, heart disease and strokes. Obese children are more likely to become obese adults and have a higher risk of developing disease, disability and premature death in adulthood (Ward et al., 2017). An issue not linked to physical health is that some pupils may experience bullying linked to their weight. Obesity is also associated with poor psychological and emotional health and poor sleep, which can impact upon a pupil's ability to learn.

In England in 2016/17, almost 25 per cent of children in Reception classes (ages five to six) were overweight or obese, an increase from 2015/16, whilst in Year 6 it was over a third, which was comparable to the previous year. Obesity prevalence was higher for boys than girls in both age groups (NHS Digital, 2017). Meanwhile, in England, 61 per cent of adults were obese (Baker, 2018); in Scotland this figure was 65 per cent (Crown copyright, 2017); in Wales 60 per cent (Welsh Government, 2018) and in Northern Ireland 63 per cent (Department of Health, 2017).

Slottje et al. (2015) suggest that school lunches add to pupils' net calorie intake and therefore may increase the probability of becoming overweight. They further contend that in younger pupils, a reduction in physical activity (such as shorter playtimes and less physical education) could lead to weight gain. In their study, von Hippel and Workman (2016) established that from the autumn of kindergarten (Year 1 in the UK) to the spring of second grade (Year 3 in the UK), the incidence of pupils' obesity increased from 8.9 per cent to 11.5 per cent, and the prevalence of being overweight increased from 23.3 per cent to 28.7 per cent. However, all of the increase occurred during the two summer vacations with no increase during any of the three school years, further demonstrating the positive influence that school and teachers can have on pupils' health and well-being.

Case Study B: The impact of exercise on weight for pupils

Country: UK

Age group: Eleven to twelve years old

Setting: Mainstream secondary school

Participants involved: Pupil B, a twelve-year-old girl, her parents, peers and class teacher

Pupil B is a girl with Down syndrome who is morbidly obese. The family takes advice from the dietician at their local hospital. Her lunch box contains very little in an attempt to manage her weight. Pupil B is included in an exchange programme to Paris, France. During the trip, she eats exactly the same food as the other pupils on the trip, but the itinerary involves increased walking. On return from the trip, it is visibly obvious that Pupil B has lost some weight, which is noticed by her parents and other staff in the school. This demonstrates the impact that a relatively small increase in the amount of exercise can have on weight management and health.

Outcomes Despite eating foods that her family perceived as contributing to weight gain, because she was active, Pupil B began to reduce her weight in a relatively short space of time.

What we can learn Pupils do not necessarily need to be involved in specific sports. They can achieve a healthy and transformative level of activity by just being more mobile. Peers and the environment can be very influential on the physically active behaviours of other pupils. Teachers should provide opportunities for pupils to be active in their learning across the curriculum.

Exercise

Hippocrates identified that 'eating alone will not keep a man well; he must also take exercise' (Jones, 1931, p. 229), while Schoenfeld et al. (2011) affirm that physical exercise reduces anxiety. The positive impact of exercise on our physical and emotional well-being is well known. According to the WHO (2018a), adults aged eighteen to sixty-four should do the following:

1. They should do at least 150 minutes of moderate-intensity aerobic physical activity throughout the week, or at least 75 minutes of vigorous-intensity aerobic physical activity throughout the week, or an equivalent combination of moderate- and vigorous-intensity activity.
2. Aerobic activity should be performed in bouts of at least ten minutes duration.
3. For additional health benefits, adults should increase their moderate-intensity aerobic physical activity to 300 minutes per week or engage in 150 minutes of vigorous-intensity aerobic physical activity per week, or an equivalent combination of moderate- and vigorous-intensity activity.
4. Muscle-strengthening activities should be done involving major muscle groups on two or more days a week.

Meanwhile, the UK Chief Medical Officers' guidelines state that children and young people aged five to eighteen years need to do sixty minutes of moderate to vigorous physical activity (MVPA) every day and that on three days a week, this activity should involve exercises to build strong muscles, like push-ups and exercises to build strong bones, such as jumping and running (Department of Health and Social Care, 2019).

Ingle and Coan (2017) confirm that children's physical activity levels are influenced by a range of factors such as friends and family and the area they live in, but they also include schools and teachers in their list. The importance of physical activity for achieving and maintaining health has been recognized for decades. Su, Wu and Su's (2018) study confirms that physical exercise positively impacts children's well-being, while Archer (2014) recommends that because of its numerous benefits to children's overall health and their learning, physical exercise should form part of any long-term health programme for children and adolescents. However, Field (2012) claims that approximately 40 per cent of school-age boys and 60 per cent of girls have not been undertaking the recommended one-hour per day of moderate-intensity physical activity. A longitudinal study in the United States by Nader et al. (2008) had similar findings. In their study, nine-year-olds engaged in MVPA for around three hours a day including weekends, but this reduced to forty-nine minutes per weekday and thirty-five minutes per day at the weekend by the time the children were fifteen years old. Nader et al. (2008) do not identify specific reasons for this decline, but it might be suggested that factors such as body image, peer pressure and possibly preparing for public exams may be relevant. As authors of this chapter, we agree with the researchers that further investigation is needed into this phenomenon as there is also evidence that participation in sport at school in the UK also decreases as pupils get older: from 64 per cent in primary school, to 40 per cent in Year 11, then 23 per cent and 21 per cent respectively in Years 12 and 13 (DfE, 2013c). This is despite outstanding Physical Education teaching being found in twice as many secondary schools as primary settings (Ofsted, 2013). The reasons for this decline in uptake do not appear to be related to teachers or teaching.

Window on research

Lord Sebastian Coe, chairman of the London Olympic Games Commission, said in 2012 that 'today's children are the least active generation in history – they also might be the first to have a shorter life expectancy than their parents' (Donnelly, 2014, webpage). In June 2015, ukactive released 'Generation Inactive', a report exploring children's physical activity in primary schools and investigating the measures used to track the activity and fitness levels of pupils. In 2018, ukactive published 'Generation Inactive 2', an update on their original report. The update aimed to provide a framework for understanding the complex and varied personal, social and environmental factors that influence pupils' engagement with physical activity.

The research adopted a qualitative methodology and data was collected via an open-ended question online consultation (which ran from 12 March to 4 June 2018) and focus groups and telephone/video conferences. Initial thematic analysis of the online consultation identified common themes, which then informed the delivery of the focus groups. Discussions were held with pupils, teachers, academics, health professionals, activity providers and then policymakers (via a parliamentary focus group). The aim of the discussions was to gain a comprehensive understanding of the factors that influence pupils' physical activity levels. The researchers received over 100 online submissions and recorded over ten hours of focus group input. The research found that pupils had reduced fitness levels following lengthy school holidays. The primary school pupils in the study lost 80 per cent of the fitness levels they had gained during term time. Moreover, the study identified marked differences in pupils from different socio-economic backgrounds, with the poorest pupils experiencing a reduction in fitness, which was eighteen times greater than that of the wealthiest. This may have been due to some families being unable to afford, and therefore access, leisure and sporting activities.

Reflective questions

1. How much time is spent in your setting/school on teaching pupils about healthy food and how to prepare it?
2. How do you help the children in your setting/school to enjoy and engage in physical exercise?

Reflexive questions

1. Reflecting on your own eating habits and behaviours, how do you ensure that you are taking good care of yourself?
2. What influences affect your approaches to taking care of your health and well-being?

Environment

There are a number of different environments that can influence pupils' or teachers' health, including their economic, political, physical or social surroundings. Looking at the economic environment, Kyttälä et al. (2014) confirm that a number of chronic disease factors including short duration of breastfeeding, unhealthy diet, inactivity and obesity are more prevalent in lower socio-economic groups. Public Health England concurs, attesting that obesity rates are highest in the most deprived 10 per cent of the population – approximately twice that of the least deprived 10 per cent (Public Health England, 2017). The prevalence gap between the most and least deprived children is widening (NHS Digital, 2017).

From a political environment perspective, the UK government has imposed budget and service cuts to universal services. Research has suggested that those parts of the country, which have borne the brunt of cuts to preventive services, are also those areas that have the greatest need. Services need to be adequately resourced if the threat to pupils' outcomes is to be averted (Crenna-Jennings, 2018). Similarly, the Institute of Fiscal Studies has reported that schools in England and Wales have endured budget cuts of 8 per cent and 5 per cent respectively, with sixth forms sustaining a reduction of 25 per cent per pupil and local authority support services a drop of 55 per cent according to Bousted (2018). On a more positive note, total spending in the early years sector has risen significantly over the last thirty years, from around £100 million in the early 1990s to £5.8 billion in 2017/18 (Bellfield, Farquharson and Sibieta, 2018). Nevertheless, Britton, Farquhason and Sibieta (2019) acknowledge that there are resource pressures across all areas of education in England, which may impact upon pupils' and teachers' well-being.

The environment in a more literal sense, that is the physical environment, is also important. Van den Bosch (2017) confirms that natural environments affect humans directly and indirectly. Not only do green and blue spaces provide opportunities for humans to interact and play, abundant urban greenery is important to health promotion since chronic stress, physical inactivity and lack of social cohesion are three major risk factors for disease (Van den Bosch, 2017). There is also some evidence of benefits to mental health for pupils who have regular access to natural environments, including a reduction in the symptoms of Attention Deficit Hyperactivity Disorder (ADHD) (Mackareth et al., 2014). Teachers need to be aware of these influences and the role they play in planning for learning that might utilize the environment for the benefit of the health and well-being of themselves and their pupils.

Increase in mental health issues

In 2017, almost 13 per cent of pupils in the UK aged five to nineteen years met the criteria for at least one mental disorder at the time of interview (NHS Digital, 2018). It is estimated that around 70 per cent of pupils who experience mental health difficulties do not receive appropriate intervention at an early enough age (Mental Health Foundation, 2018). Furthermore, research has shown a significant increase in mental health difficulties experienced by children and young people (Frith, 2016). The number of young people aged under eighteen attending Accident and Emergency departments in hospitals because of a psychiatric condition has more than doubled between 2010 and 2015, and referrals to specialist child and adolescent mental health services (CAMHS) increased by 64 per cent between 2012/13 and 2014/15 (Earle, 2016). Moreover, 50 per cent of mental illness in adult life (excluding dementia) starts before age fifteen and 75 per cent by age eighteen. The risk of mental disorder increases with age, with rates at the highest in girls aged seventeen to nineteen years (NHS Digital, 2018). Nevertheless, in any class of thirty pupils, teachers are statistically likely to encounter at least two with an emotional disorder and one with a behavioural or conduct disorder. Hyperactivity disorder is reported to account for one in sixty children and young people aged five to nineteen years and eating disorder or autism one in fifty children (NHS Digital, 2018).

While it is extremely rewarding, teaching may also be stressful for some. Research has suggested that teachers can report higher than average levels of physical and mental ill health and lower than average levels of job satisfaction than in other professions (Herman, Hickmon-Rosa and Reinke, 2018). Factors that contribute to teacher stress include: workload, expectations, accountability and lack of support. Those with the longest number of years of service are most likely to report low levels of stress, with 53 per cent of those with thirty-one plus years of service saying they do not feel stressed compared with 30 per cent of those with just one to five years (Education Support Partnership, 2017). This implies that teachers who are new to the profession need access to the right kinds of support to enable them to transition successfully from trainee to teacher and that, given that appropriate support, they can flourish in their chosen career.

How might teachers be supported in accessing services for themselves?

Supervision is well established in professions like nursing and social work. Increasingly, people who work in schools are managing complex situations which pupils face. Therefore, teachers could benefit from receiving regular supervision. In that context its functions would include:

- developing practice (through reflection), producing confident, autonomous practitioners;
- managing the psychological and emotional impact of work and reducing time taken off work through stress-related illness;
- improving staff retention;
- highlighting issues that require an organizational or policy response; and
- ensuring that pupils continue to receive high-quality teaching (Reid and Westergaard, 2013 cited in Westergaard and Bainbridge, 2014).

Westergaard and Bainbridge (2014) agree that those working with pupils in schools should have access to quality supervision but point out that they do not mean the type of supervision that has managerial- or performance-related connotations. They confirm that a supervisor is not a mentor, a counsellor or a manager, but an independent professional and advocate whom the teacher meets three times a term for at least an hour, to enable a safe and trusting relationship to develop. Reid (in Reid, Westergaard and Claringbull, 2013) confirms that supervision is not a therapy.

Teachers aspire to be reflective practitioners and Reid (2013) endorses that a reflective practitioner is able to reach potential solutions by analysing their experience and prior knowledge, to inform current and future practice (see Chapter 8). Supervision is aimed at facilitating that process.

Launer (2018) defines interprofessional supervision as being when someone from one profession supervises a colleague from another. He acknowledges that this usually happens across professions in healthcare, but effective interprofessional practice could take place across health, social care and education – a view founded upon Lord Laming's review into the death of Victoria Climbié and mandated in statutory guidance such as *Working Together to Safeguard Children* (DfE, 2018). Paterson and Grantham (2016) confirm that educational psychologists (EPs) are in a unique position to model and promote emotional literacy (the ability to understand and express feelings appropriately) in all school relationships. There may be the potential for them to be instrumental in implementing or facilitating supervision for teachers.

In the absence of supervision as described by Westergaard and Bainbridge (2014), teachers can look after their health and well-being and be supported by establishing relationships with colleagues, as a community of support (which is discussed more fully in Chapter 7). By adopting an interprofessional approach to their practice, that is to say collaborating not only with other teachers/professionals at their school, but also with colleagues at other schools (e.g. through their NQT training programme, or Multi Academy Trust INSET days), they can also be supported in accessing services for themselves, children and families. 'Collaboration among a wide variety of educational professionals is essential to the effectiveness of any school, and thus to the learning and well-being of the students in that school' (Dobbs-Oates and Morris, 2014, p. 50).

Window on research

According to Herman, Hickmon-Rosa and Reinke (2018, p. 90), 'Understanding how teacher stress, burnout, coping, and self-efficacy are interrelated can inform preventive and intervention efforts to support teachers.' Their study explored these ideas to determine their relationship to student outcomes, including disruptive behaviour and academic achievement. Participants in this study were 121 teachers and 1,817 students from kindergarten to fourth grade (which is Year 1 to Year 5 in England), from nine elementary schools in an urban Midwestern school district of the United States of America. Four profiles of teacher adjustment were identified. Three classes were characterized by high levels of stress and were distinguished by variations in coping and burnout ranging from (a) high coping/low burnout (60 per cent) to (b) moderate coping and burnout (30 per cent), to (c) low coping/high burnout (3 per cent). The fourth class was distinguished by low stress, high coping and low burnout. Only 7 per cent of the sample fell into this Well Adjusted class. Teachers in the high-stress, high-burnout and low-coping class were associated with the poorest student outcomes (Herman, Hickmon-Rosa and Reinke, 2018, p. 90). Bower and Carroll (2017) agree that teacher well-being is linked to student outcomes.

Reflective questions

1. What could you do in your school or classroom to influence pupils' eating habits? What are the cultural and religious factors that you would need to consider?
2. What issues might affect children and families' mental health in your school?
3. What issues might affect your mental health?
4. What mechanisms or services are provided to support teachers' health and well-being in your setting?
5. Read the Marmot (2010) review into health equalities in England or latest census data and consider how they might inform strategies to support pupils' health and well-being in your school.

Reflexive questions

1. What factors impact upon your, or your pupils', motivation or ability to take physical exercise, look after your mental health and eat healthily?
2. How might they be addressed?

Implications for teachers

Parents play an important role in helping their children to develop good habits relating to healthy eating and physical activity. They are also critical in helping their overweight or even obese children to lose weight successfully (Rhee, McEachern and Jelalian, 2014). Ofsted (2018, p. 10) asserts that 'there are too many factors beyond the school gate that make this impossible for [teachers] to control' but nevertheless acknowledges that the contribution schools can make in educating and supporting children and parents in order to tackle childhood obesity is extremely important.

There continues to be inequality in health in the UK in a range of areas, some of which are mentioned in this chapter; however, Lewis and Lenehan (2014) agree that health is everyone's business across the whole children and young people's workforce. Educating the entire workforce including teachers is vital in prevention work for all aspects of health and well-being.

The transition period from trainee to teacher may be a stage when teachers are especially vulnerable to mental health difficulties according to McLean et al. (2017), making it especially important that new teachers have access to mentorship, professional advocates and support that is meaningful. This could include interprofessional supervision, which would enable teachers to reflect on knowledge and experience, facilitated by someone with whom they have developed a safe and trusting professional relationship. Seeking appropriate support may facilitate a teacher's growth as an effective practitioner and reduce the risk of stress-related illness and burnout, which has been shown to impact negatively on pupils' learning, development and attainment in education.

Reflective questions

As a professional how do you engage with the core themes of this chapter:

1. that the health and well-being of pupils have impact upon their holistic development and progress in learning and
2. that the health and well-being of teachers have impact upon pupils' holistic development and progress in learning

Reflexive question

As a professional how do you engage with these core themes in relation to your own emotions and assumptions and biases?

Annotated bibliography

Marmot, M. (2010). *Fair society, healthy lives.* Available at: http://www. instituteofhealthequity.org/resources-reports/fair-society-healthy-lives-the-marmot-review/fair-society-healthy-lives-full-report-pdf.pdf.
This report identifies inequalities in health, which persist in twenty-first-century England, despite attempts by successive governments to address the gap. Its remit includes making

recommendations on possible strategies, which could be implemented. One of the report's key findings was that health inequalities are largely preventable, but that they are determined by a series of factors including housing, income, education, social isolation and disability. The report identifies that education has a responsibility to support action on addressing health inequalities.

Thorburn, M. (ed.) (2018). *Wellbeing, education and contemporary schooling*. Abingdon: Routledge.

This book examines well-being in schools and argues that it should be integral to core policy objectives in both health and education. The whole school focus enhances the review of well-being in schools and supports teachers to understand the complex relationships between learners and teachers, where every teacher has a responsibility for learners' well-being. By exploring a range of debates about the nature of well-being, the book shows how a child's well-being is inseparable from their overall capacity to learn and achieve, and to become confident, self-assured and active citizens.

ukactive (2018). *Generation inactive 2*. Available at: https://www.ukactive.com/wp-content/uploads/2018/09/Generation_Inactive-2_Nothing_About_Us_Without_Us.pdf.

This research (which is described in the chapter) identified seventeen recommendation areas for individuals, their social connections, organizations, communities and broader public policy to create the conditions in which our children can flourish. The recommendations are intended to help empower (amongst others) head teachers to tackle children's inactivity.

4

Child Development

Rowena Passy and Martin Gilchrist

Introduction

Child development is a complex, many-faceted area (Doherty and Hughes, 2009) that concerns physical and psychological progression from the dependence that is experienced in infancy and early childhood towards more mature competence and adulthood (Woodhead, 2006). It involves children of all ages making sense of and negotiating their way through their world; there is now an understanding that they are not passive recipients of socialization but active meaning-makers who engage at different levels with the social, cultural and physical world around them (Littleton, 2005). And it is important to recognize that although child development can be divided into different areas such as physical, cognitive and socio-emotional, the experience of human development is holistic, and that the different aspects of development all contribute to the people that we become.

This chapter argues that the strength of outdoor learning is that it addresses different aspects of children's development holistically, mirroring the child's overall developmental experience. Let us take school gardening as an example, in which children's physical, cognitive and socio-emotional development can be supported through the simple acts of digging, weeding, planting, tending and harvesting. Such physical activity encourages the development of both gross (e.g. digging) and fine (e.g. weeding) motor skills, which can help to guard against obesity – a lack of physical skills is a factor that contributes to this condition (Doherty and Hughes, 2009) – while the exercise associated with the task keeps children physically active. Interest in the garden produce can contribute to healthy eating habits; children are more likely to eat new and/or different fruits and vegetables that they have grown, and using garden crops in the school canteen can contribute to a school-wide healthy living culture (Page, Bremner and Passy, 2017). Cognitive development can be encouraged through practical problem-solving – how many courgette plants would fit in this plot? – as well as through more academic pursuits such as experimenting with different growing techniques and learning about the different wildlife attracted to the garden area. Finally, socio-emotional development is encouraged through the collective act of maintaining a garden; children have to work together to complete the range of different tasks, to nurture young plants and then share the results of their efforts. Resilience is needed to withstand vandalism on the school grounds and the disappointment of crops failing; confidence grows through perseverance and success through healthy plants; children learn responsibility through the act of cultivation (Passy, Reed and Morris, 2010). Briefly put, outdoor learning activities such as gardening can offer a rounded opportunity for child development that is impossible indoors.

Reflective questions

1. In what ways do you think outdoor learning can support children's holistic development?
2. Does it vary depending on the age of the child?

In what follows, and drawing on the experience of the Natural Connections Demonstration Project (NCDP), we examine ways in which outdoor learning can become embedded in a school's everyday practices in ways that encourage children's development. In the window on research, we describe the project. We then illustrate the ways in which project schools supported three broad areas of child development – socio-emotional, physical and cognitive – through outdoor learning. While we focus on these aspects separately, our analysis is underpinned by the idea of holistic development presented above; outdoor learning activities within this project tended to encourage physical activity and different kinds of social interaction, and there was generally some kind of targeted practical or curricular-led learning in the outdoor sessions. We then discuss the challenges encountered during the project and ways in which schools overcame them to embed a culture of outdoor learning in their schools. Finally, we reflect on how outdoor learning can be adopted in any school that has the necessary collective will to do so.

Window on research

Waite, S., Passy, R., Gilchrist, M., Hunt, A. and Blackwell, I. (2016). *natural connections demonstration project, 2012–2016: Final report*. Natural England commissioned reports, Number 215. Available at: http://publications. naturalengland.org.uk/publication/6636651036540928.

The long-term aim of the initiative outlined in *The Natural Choice* White Paper (HM Government, 2011) was to enable all children within England to benefit from learning experiences in their local natural environments. The Natural Connections Demonstration Project (NCDP) was intended to be the first phase of realizing this ambition. It aimed to develop understanding of what was needed to engage schools with outdoor learning and enable a culture change within schools in which teachers could embrace both the concept and the practice of taking learning outside. If successful in both stimulating and meeting the apparent latent demand in schools (Rickinson et al., 2012), it was intended that the project lessons could be replicated and amplified more widely and that subsequent phases might have different foci such as outdoor play or health outcomes. The project findings have informed the grant competition for Nature Friendly Schools, a new £6.4 million programme that is aimed at improving children's well-being, learning and care for the environment through learning outdoors (https://www.wildlifetrusts.org/news/new-nature-friendly-schools).

NCDP was a four-year project (2012 to 2016) funded by the Department for the Environment, Food and Rural Affairs (DEFRA), Natural England and Historic England, and delivered by a team at the University of Plymouth. Responding to the White Paper, the project model was informed by research commissioned by Natural England on teacher and school leader views on (Rickinson et al., 2012) and the barriers to and the benefits of (Dillon and Dickie, 2012) learning outside the classroom in natural environments. The model conceived as a result of this research was one of local independent brokerage of outdoor learning services to schools, which would be supported by local volunteers and what was originally thought of as a 'one-stop shop' website. Information provided by the independent brokers could range across the spectrum of possible services including grounds development, continuing professional development (CPD) and outdoor learning consultancy as well as providing the opportunity to connect with other schools and teachers; volunteers would support teachers outside either as specialists for particular subject areas or as an extra pair of hands; the website would provide immediate and accessible information for teachers on all stages of their outdoor learning practice. The intention was to build belief in the benefits of outdoor learning, together with the skills and confidence to provide outdoor learning for pupils rather than rely on external support.

Implementation of the project was aimed at building local networks in five areas or 'hubs'. Local brokerage agencies, or 'hub leaders', recruited, then supported and enhanced the work of schools that were already successfully engaging with outdoor learning. Once staff in the first wave of recruited schools felt confident enough in their own practice, they, together with their hub leaders, began to recruit other schools and set up local networks of support. The five hub leaders came from different organizations and professional backgrounds connected with outdoor learning, and were located in different areas across the south-west of England. Altogether they worked in different ways with around 130 schools in exploring, experimenting with and developing outdoor learning (Waite et al., 2016).

The delivery team decided to focus the project on curricular learning, as this would enable schools to absorb different practices and pedagogies into their everyday activity and would align with schools' responsibility of ensuring that children were taught the different components of the national curriculum. It also had the added consideration that schools were more likely to buy into a project that worked with the grain of the current system, for teachers were unlikely to consider undertaking new and/or extra work that was unconnected to curricular requirements, something confirmed through project findings. Schools were invited to join the project and to develop their own outdoor learning practice in a way that fitted their priorities and their staff wishes, with the result that outdoor learning practice appeared in very different forms across the project. Schools involved some, most or all of their staff, and outdoor learning was used for all curricular areas, although most regularly and consistently in the core subjects of science, English and maths as well as physical education (Waite et al., 2016).

An extensive evaluation was carried out during the project implementation time; data collected included 3,083 survey returns (from fifteen different surveys to schools, volunteers, outdoor learning providers, pupils and parents), thirty-five semi-structured interviews with hub leaders and twenty-four case-study visits to schools. Semi-structured interviews were conducted during these school visits with 119 school staff, 11 volunteers and 167 pupils (Waite et al., 2016, p. 25). All quotations in what follows are unattributed to maintain schools' and individuals' anonymity.

Supporting children's socio-emotional development

In the final project survey that was sent to schools, participants were asked to respond to the question: 'Do you feel that learning outside in the natural environment has had an impact on your pupils' social skills?' Respondents could select from 'positive impact', 'no impact', 'negative impact' and 'don't know' (Gilchrist et al., 2017a, p. 82), and 93 per cent (81/87) agreed that it had a positive impact (Gilchrist et al., 2017b, p. 163). This response was sustained by interviewees in our case study visits, who all spoke of the importance of outdoor learning to socio-emotional development; teachers consistently reported that children's levels of communication and self-management improved when they were outside during school time, and that this had a positive effect on pupils' confidence and self-esteem. This progression related to two broad affordances of outdoor learning: offering children a wider range of learning opportunities, which we discuss in more detail under 'physical' and 'cognitive' development, and changing the nature of children's relationships with both peers and adults through different approaches to learning. This is illustrated below.

Window on practice

Changing relationships through different approaches to learning

The lead teacher in one special school recognized the value of outdoor learning through his experience in residential schools, arguing that it gave children the time and the space to work differently with adults who provided their care. Another teacher at the same school explained that her passion was to encourage the children to develop relationships with animals because children 'have a natural attraction to animals … they learn to externalise their feelings through the animals' which, in turn, helped the children to understand themselves and then to develop their own ability to communicate with both peers and adults. She recounted how the goal of the admissions team was to encourage children's relationship-building.

Interaction with peers and adults is an important part of children's development, as it helps to increase their understanding of, and ability to participate in, the social world in which they live (Littleton and Miell, 2005). Many of the pupils in this school had experienced failure in mainstream schools and were unable to cope with large groups of children in a classroom. Teachers in this school believed that pupils first needed to be able to maintain eye contact as a precursor to managing a one-to-one relationship; that managing a one-to-one relationship was an essential foundation to managing a group relationship; and that collaboration over, say, a piece of geography was only possible at this point. One teacher told us that their work was therefore about '*understanding the children from their early steps* [in the school], *building their confidence, building their experiences, building their language skills*' and that '*these things can be delivered better by going outside*'. During the course of our visit, they gave us several examples of the ways in which children changed the nature of their relationships with others through activities outdoors, including the following:

Teachers spoke of one boy, whose '*presentation was always very sullen, quite depressed,* [you] *never saw him smile. But put him on the end of a lead with one of the dogs and he'd laugh, he'd giggle, he'd skip, he'd run about and you saw a totally different side to the child*'. On the strength of this obvious enjoyment, he was given the opportunity to go horse riding, which had much the same effect on his behaviour. These encounters with animals meant that he started to '*warm. And then he'd start to have conversations. And we learnt a lot more about him'.* As the boy became *'much more engageable',* he could begin to form new relationship patterns with both staff and fellow pupils. And staff had found a way to support him when he *'went to the dark place';* one of the things that *'brought him round'* was being with the animals.

Another boy in the same school found the classroom environment highly stressful and difficult but, when he was taken outside, staff found that he was *'a born leader. He can really help the other kids that maybe don't necessarily … want to get … involved'.* His teacher explained that Forest School *'raises his confidence. And the other children who see him in a different light too. He also becomes more engaged and inquisitive'.* This gave him *'a bit more kudos'* with his peers, as well as *'pride and self-confidence'* because he was experiencing success in the activities he was undertaking and because others were gaining positive feedback about him. As his teacher commented, *'every child needs success and sometimes you need to change the environment to enable that';* while the indoor classroom was difficult for this child, he was able to shine in these outdoor activities with the result that his peers and teachers saw him in a different light. As was the case with the boy who improved his communication through animals, these activities enabled this young man to engage in more positive relationships with adults and peers in his school.

Many other case study teachers commented on the way that outdoor learning changed the nature of school relationships. One Assistant Head Teacher in a secondary school believed that taking young people outside enabled teachers to see them respond to learning in a different way. Children may demonstrate 'funds of knowledge' (Moll et al., 1992, p. 132) in particular areas that the teacher knew nothing about, engage with more enthusiasm than usual with the task in hand or demonstrate new learning, all of which can generate teachers' respect for individual pupils. A primary school teacher suggested that, when outside, some children

> *are able to relax and don't feel the pressure they might in class … I think they do really well, through thinking differently and* [they] *seem more relaxed outside for some reason. A lot of the children who are very anxious when they are asked to do a task in the classroom, ask them to do the same task outside … they seem more relaxed and more able to engage with it.*

There is an increasing body of evidence that green areas can have a calming and relaxing effect (e.g. DEFRA et al., 2017; Gill, 2014), and the combination of the physical and mental space when outside may contribute to these noticeable changes in children and young people's attitudes and behaviour. But children can see their teachers in a different way, too – an idea expressed by a primary school teacher who reported relationship changes from the children's point of view:

> *The children actually look at teachers differently after they have been on these* [outdoor] *sessions, because they are no longer just the person at the front just pointing and telling them, they are actually doing things with them … So it becomes a different relationship.*

The activities described in this section link to children's physical development through, for example, riding a pony, walking the dog or building camps in a Forest School session. In the next section we focus on how outdoor learning has been used to encourage children's physical development.

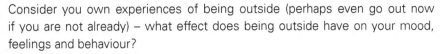

Reflective question

Consider you own experiences of being outside (perhaps even go out now if you are not already) – what effect does being outside have on your mood, feelings and behaviour?

Supporting children's physical development

A frequent comment from case study school teachers was that children nowadays have fewer opportunities to play outside than they did; a typical remark was that taking learning outside in school time was

> about children taking risks and actually being able to manage those risks and assess [them] … Nowadays we have taken away … the danger … The only danger they can have now is a virtual danger through their Xboxes … Gone are the days when children can go out and play in woods all day like I used to.

This teacher believed that there was an absence of physical risk in many young people's lives, and she linked this with the physical freedom that she thought had been lost in recent generations, a subject investigated in research commissioned in 2009 by Natural England. This research report suggested that children spent less time playing in natural places such as woodlands and countryside than their parents or grandparents; under 10 per cent of children reported playing in natural places, in comparison to 40 per cent of their parents and grandparents who reported playing in such areas when they were children (England Marketing, 2009, p. 8). The report also suggested that more children would like to play in natural spaces and that more parents would like them to do so. Equally, other research shows how a growth in urbanization, changes in work and transport patterns, plus a fear of strangers and the lure of on-screen entertainment can lead to an increasingly sedentary lifestyle (see Page, Bremner and Passy, 2017 for an overview). In turn, this suggests that schools can be a critically important place for children to play and learn outside: to develop their physical skills, to learn about risk management, to experience the physical freedom of earlier generations and, at the same time, to learn about the natural world. This was a point reiterated by many of the project case study head teachers.

One of the main opportunities for physical development can be Forest School. Almost all NCDP case study schools used Forest School (e.g. Knight, 2011) as part of their outdoor learning offer, adapted in different ways to suit their circumstances and priorities. Several had large enough grounds to accommodate weekly Forest School sessions, while others travelled to a site organized by others or brought in trained Forest School leaders to run activities. An important foundation of the NCDP project was supporting schools to make their grounds suitable for the types of outdoor learning that the teachers wanted to undertake, and some developed Forest School areas within their grounds during the project lifetime. Sessions were used to provide children with opportunities such as playing with rope swings, rope bridges and building dens; collecting berries and making jam; climbing trees and making rafts; making hot chocolate and toasting marshmallows; and using tools to make wooden items for sale at the school Christmas fair. These different activities helped in different ways to develop children's gross and fine motor skills, their balance, their physical awareness of danger and how risk can be managed, all while enjoying and absorbing information about the natural world around them.

One innovative case study primary school developed an approach that combined curricular learning and the ethos of Forest School with the maintenance of their extensive grounds in a way that was practical, enjoyable and made a major contribution to the school community.

Window on practice

Physical activity and grounds maintenance: A 'win-win' solution

The problem cited by the outdoor learning lead was that the maintenance of the school's grounds had become *'a real worry'* because of their size and maturity; the site had a large number of trees (due to the native planting tree scheme that was active when the school was built a few decades before), a nature area with a boardwalk alongside a stream and a variety of discrete areas around the grounds that included a vegetable garden, a space for chickens, different copses, a large field and a Forest School area. While all interviewees agreed that the site was *'stunning'*, there was equal agreement that its maintenance was highly time-consuming and that finding volunteers to help on a regular basis was a challenge.

The outdoor lead's solution was to engage in the John Muir Award with Year 6 pupils (aged ten to eleven), Year 6 teachers and a group of initial teacher education students on placement from a local university. Each year, during a week in February, the children would have their daily maths lesson and then the school timetable was suspended so that they could spend their time outside undertaking the four John Muir Award elements of Discover, Explore, Conserve and Share (see https://www.johnmuirtrust.org/john-muir-award). Together, the teachers, students and children would:

Discover

- The university students provided high adult/child ratios to allow the children to discover places on the school site that they had not seen before.

Explore

- These were mainly Forest School or arts activities. The university students planned activities in advance and ran them all over the site, so the children were able to engage in new experiences such as conservation or earth education activities.

Conserve

- This was the biggest part of the week, in which the children undertook a lot of the physical work of grounds maintenance. Projects were planned in a walk before the week to generate ideas and then chosen by the children. In the year that we visited the school, conservation projects included:
  - Maintaining the boardwalk and replacing the eighty-six planks that had either rotted or been vandalized in that year.
  - Pond tidying, clearing and maintaining. This included re-laying the woodchip surface around the pond, so it could continue to be a complete learning environment.
  - Making wooden hurdles to screen an area of rubbish. Children harvested the hazel that was to be used for the hurdles from the school grounds, and an NCDP grant paid for a hurdle maker to work with the students and children for the day.
  - Clearing paths and re-laying woodchip paths. The school had contacts with local tree surgeons to supply the woodchip.
  - Monitoring and repairing old bird boxes, and making new ones.
  - Weeding the vegetable garden and putting woodchip around the area to make it a useable space for the rest of the year.

Share

- The Year 6 children held an assembly before the week started, explaining what they were going to do and sharing their 'record books' with the parents who attended. During the week, pupils shared artwork and some recording with the other pupils. When the week was over they created displays and models, made cakes with a themed decoration and constructed a display board, which was hung up in the school foyer as a legacy.

As can be imagined, this week was regarded as the high spot of the year by Year 6 pupils, and the outdoor learning lead commented that she had always found that all children enjoyed the experience. When we spoke with some of the children involved, they talked about relishing the physical tasks that involved using axes, saws and mallets, and of their pleasure and pride in learning how to look after the school grounds. Their extension of this experience, evident when they discussed *'learning to look after the environment'*, suggests that building a relationship with their local area helps young people to understand the importance of caring in a more general way for nature and the environment (Louv, 2008).

Supporting children's cognitive development

Earlier we argued that taking learning outside offers children a wider range of learning opportunities than in the classroom, and we have already seen how schools have used different spaces and foci to support children's socio-emotional and physical development. In this section we focus on the cognitive development offered by the outdoors. This is a wide area that includes decision making, memory and critical and creative thinking; learning is an important part (Doherty and Hughes, 2009), while curricular learning is at the heart of the school obligation in England to enable children and young people to access 'a curriculum which is balanced and broadly based' and which

promotes the spiritual, moral, cultural, mental and physical development of pupils at the school and of society prepares pupils at the school for the opportunities, responsibilities and experiences of later life.

(DfE, 2014, p. 5)

In the project survey responses, and using the same response alternatives of 'positive impact', 'no impact', 'negative impact' and 'don't know', 95 per cent of responding teachers (83/87) agreed that outdoor learning had a positive effect on pupils' enjoyment of lessons. Ninety-two per cent (80/87) agreed that it had a positive effect on pupils' engagement with learning (Gilchrist et al., 2017b, p. 163). During the case study interviews, participants spoke of the *'real life'* opportunities that outdoor learning gave children to learn, and how this gave a *'purpose'* to their school work that made learning meaningful. As one primary school teacher commented, outdoor learning

does help the children to see the benefit of what we are doing ... why you have to learn about doing long multiplication that they can't see the relevance of beyond their maths book. It does help them to apply it in a way [that] ... gives it real purpose.

In many cases giving purpose to children's school work involved teachers being imaginative in the way that they presented tasks; examples included learning about Roger Bannister's achievement of running a four-minute mile, in which the class calculated the number of lengths of track required for them to run a mile in relay during class time, and then ran the mile. Another example concerned investigating a UFO (unidentified flying object) that had landed in the school grounds; in this case the Teaching Assistant was dressed up as an alien, so the class could interview her and write a news report. A third involved the topic of castles, in which pupils first discussed what was needed for a castle site, and then split into two groups to choose an area in the school grounds: one selected the higher ground and the other the lower. The pupils then spent the day learning strategies of attacking each other, in a way that involved plenty of water!

Teachers also talked about enabling different types of learning from the abstract approach that is often a significant part of the classroom experience:

> From an educational perspective it [outdoor learning] can be really valuable ... Because often the nature of outdoor learning is very practical, it's very kinaesthetic. And so for a lot of children that is really useful and that can ... secure learning and understanding that something more paper based, more oral or visual ... might not work for them.

One example of this type of learning came from a primary school teacher, who taught children about river processes such as meandering and flooding by putting gravel and sand on a path and pouring water onto the paths. Her comment was that 'this is the sort of thing they [pupils] need to be doing ... rather than a worksheet, where they have got to label things; [that is] a closed procedure that is not open-ended enough'. Similarly, a secondary school teacher enthused about taking science lessons outside, saying that

> one of the key bits of the science curriculum is the wonderment of science. I think it is hard to bring in the wonderment of science stuck in a science lab for the whole year, whereas if you get outside you can give some people a real 'Oh my gosh!'
>
> (Waite et al., 2016, p. 67)

While some of these activities needed adequate space on the school grounds, others took place on more limited areas. Plants were used to inspire poetry, for example, and it is possible to put tubs for growing vegetables and/or flowers on any reasonably flat surface. Similarly, neglected corners can be brought into use as an environmental area or a space for quiet reflection, and it is not necessary to be outside for a whole lesson; project teachers spoke of how they could go outside for a short period, for example, to set up a lesson and then return indoors. Some schools had the good fortune to be located near open spaces such as woods, beaches or parks, and would use these spaces on a regular basis. Devising a blanket risk assessment that covered any areas to which the children walked minimized administrative processes and gave everyone more time to be outside. A few project schools had farms as part of their premises, and below we describe how the farm's development and management were used as learning opportunities for pupils in one primary school.

Case study: Practical problems to solve – farming as part of primary school life

Country: England

Age group: Eight to eleven

Setting: Primary school

Participants involved: Head teacher, teacher, pupils

The head teacher of this school had a strong belief that children enjoyed being outside and that the quality of their work improved when they had real-life examples to work on. She argued that outdoor learning 'brings most curriculum areas alive' and encouraged teachers to take their classes outside at least twice a week.

Each year, the Key Stage 2 pupils (aged eight to eleven) took on a particular project that supported the management and development of the farm. The latest had been focused on building a donkey shelter. Pupils were asked to work out the size that was needed and then to make a scaled drawing of the proposed shelter. When this was completed, pupils created a budget, emailed different companies to arrange site meetings and developed a detailed implementation plan; they presented this to the governors, who gave permission for the project to go ahead. The teacher commented that the 'higher purpose' of the project – to ensure that the donkey could be warm and dry – meant that there was 'a higher quality literacy and numeracy' in the work that the children were doing. In addition to this, presenting their case to the governors meant the pupils had to develop a clear rationale for the project and demonstrate that they were able to complete it satisfactorily, thereby encouraging teamwork, presentation skills and public speaking.

Other successful projects at this school included pupils negotiating good-value willow workshops for all year groups, sourcing a model cow that could be 'milked', installing water pipes for the farm area, and selling vegetables and meat from the farm at the school shop. Half of the funds raised from the sales went to an African charity, and the other half to purchase seeds for future gardening endeavours – although in one year these funds were supplemented by children either writing or making phone calls to local suppliers, asking them to donate seeds for the school's growing areas. These efforts were well-rewarded; their teacher commented that, once the children had the confidence to make the calls, the results were *'surprising … they are very difficult to say no to!'*.

Conclusion: Embedding outdoor learning in schools

Although we have divided the case study data into three areas of child development, the activities we have described were rarely focused entirely on one aspect but encouraged a holistic approach; physical and cognitive challenges were combined in different ways with socio-emotional learning. Teacher interviewees believed that the variety of tasks and challenges when outside gave all children who participated an opportunity to succeed in some way, giving them greater overall confidence. In their review of non-cognitive skills, Gutman and Schoon (2013) argue that confidence and self-esteem 'appear to be an essential precursor to enhancing other non-cognitive skills' or, to put it another way, that children tend to be reluctant to try learning new skills or to attempt new activities unless they believe they can succeed (Gutman and Schoon, 2013, p. 11). Our case study interviewees placed great value on the growth of children's confidence, and this suggests that they would agree with Gutman and Schoon's views in a way that can be summed up as: taking learning outdoors offers an holistic approach to child development that encourages children to become confident, independent learners who are able to face new challenges.

We would caution, however, that merely taking a lesson outdoors does not improve its quality; as one of the hub leaders commented, teachers need to make sure that they are adding value to a lesson by taking it outside – *'just doing it outside is not good enough'*. This means that lessons need to be planned carefully, ensuring that the aims and objectives are as clear as for any lesson indoors and that the task in hand is one that will work better outside than inside. There needs to be an understanding, too, that the space and the nature of tasks outside will require a different pedagogy as both teachers and children adjust to greater freedom of movement and a wider range of tasks.

While most challenges to outdoor learning during the NCDP were school-specific, there were two main barriers to embedding outdoor learning into schools' everyday working life. The first related to teacher confidence. NCDP research found that teachers needed time to develop their own confidence in taking lessons outside and that CPD was an essential part of supporting this process. Relevant, high-quality CPD developed staff knowledge, understanding and practice of outdoor learning, and helped individual schools to address practical challenges such as funding, grounds development and health and safety requirements. As part of this process, teachers reported that they valued meeting up with colleagues from other schools to compare their approaches, problem-solving methods and lesson plans. A substantial majority of project teachers believed that the time taken to develop their outdoor learning expertise was well-spent; in their end-of-project survey responses 79 per cent (68/86) of responding teachers agreed that outdoor learning had a positive impact on teaching practice, while 72 per cent (62/86) agreed that it had a positive impact on teachers' health and well-being, and 69 per cent (60/86) agreed that teachers' professional development and job satisfaction were improved through outdoor learning. As one teacher commented, outdoor learning 'feeds the soul'.

The second challenge related to the lack of time, which was closely related to the degree of pressure that any school might feel to produce strong examination results. Although one hub leader reported that a school placed in the Ofsted category 'inadequate' had used outdoor learning as an important part of their improvement strategy, the more usual reaction was to draw back from these activities with the intention of teaching core subjects inside. Conversely, schools with high Ofsted grades could feel at greater liberty to introduce new ways of working in their schools than those with lower grades (Gilchrist et al., 2017b, pp. 185, 200). Finding a way though these issues depended largely on the extent to which the head teacher and senior leadership team provided practical and moral support for outdoor learning. Important aspects of this included ensuring outdoor learning was written into school policy documents, providing adequate resources (including staff time) to plan new lessons, ensuring the outdoor learning lead was a respected member of staff and encouraging teachers to take their lessons outside. 'Fab Fridays', no-electricity or empty classroom days, or simply making clear the expectation that all teachers should take at least one lesson outside per week were all successful ways of encouraging outdoor learning by project head teachers. Equally, however, staff needed to be open-minded about the ways in which teaching outside can support children's development, prepared to take risks in trying new ways of teaching and to take time to build their expertise. To summarize, embedding outdoor learning as part of everyday working life depended on the collective will of the school staff, a supportive school ethos and a generous pinch of goodwill from all involved.

Reflective questions

1. As a professional how do you engage with the core themes of this chapter:
2. the role of outdoor learning in supporting children's holistic development,
3. having the confidence to adopt different outdoor learning practices and
4. adopting a whole school approach to outdoor learning.

Reflexive question

As a professional how do you engage with these core themes in relation to your own emotions and assumptions and biases?

Annotated bibliography

Passy, R. (2014). 'School gardens: Teaching and learning outside the front door', *Education 3–13*, 42(1), pp. 23–38.

This article draws on two projects, one that explores the impact of school gardens on the learning of primary school children and a second that looks at pedagogy in the garden. While the garden is seen to being able to support children's learning, teacher's willingness to use it is a factor.

Waite, S., Passy, R., Gilchrist, M., Hunt, A. and Blackwell, I. (2016). *Natural connections demonstration project, 2012–2016: Final report*. Natural England Commissioned Reports, Number 215. Available at: http://publications. naturalengland.org.uk/publication/6636651036540928

This is the full report of the research project that forms the basis of the chapter. The report emphasizes the positive impact of outdoor learning for educators and pupil, while highlighting the importance of support from school leadership teams and open-mindedness as facilitative factors in developing outdoor learning.

5

Technology Education

James Bettany with Rebecca
Smallshaw and Declan Barney

Introduction

'Digital technologies are doing for human brainpower what the steam engine and related technologies did for human muscle power during the Industrial Revolution.' (McAfee, 2015)

Children live in a technology-rich world. Whether educators should allow that to extend into school or make school a place protected from the distractions of technology is the subject of much debate. As with any complex and contested topic, there is no simple answer. The aim of this chapter is to reflect on the use of technology in learning settings. It is not intended to dictate one particular approach or way of thinking. Rather, the aim is to equip those working in education to think about the impact of the technology available and to make decisions that are the best ones for the children in the setting and/or community, and that will facilitate the teaching and learning experiences. Conrad Gesner was a respected academic with several well-received publications to his name. In discussing new communications technology, he expressed considerable concern. Gesner believed that new technology would lead to people being overloaded with information and to a loss of cognitive abilities as a result. The technology he was concerned about was the printing press and he was writing in the year 1545. Such wariness of change is well recognized through the ages, with the adoption of new ideas and their diffusion into everyday practice being a slow and delicate process (Rogers, 2003). Even Aristotle warned that writing would create forgetfulness because students would cease to exercise their capacity to remember (Plato, trans. 1925).

Adding to that, the idea that trivial information might outcompete significant information, and retaining unimportant information may limit room for ideas, remains a concern in an age of limitless access to recorded media (Gabler, 2011). Such warnings, and the longer history of caution in relation to new technologies, highlight the responsibility of teachers to equip learners to be thoughtful and critical users of technology (Parsons, 2012, p. 54) so that they avoid potential pitfalls and instead draw meaningful learning from their experiences.

The current changes in technology and their societal impact have been termed the fourth industrial revolution with big data and smart devices predicted to drive fundamental changes to business and manufacturing (Gilchrist, 2016). It is not possible to make perfect predictions of the future but a fair assumption is that children will be ever more influenced by technological innovations and they will work in a jobs market where technology has created myriad new roles while making others obsolete (Autor, Levy and Murnane, 2003).

The message here is that technology brings about change, but human beings are constant. Good pedagogy will always be good pedagogy. Good teachers will be those who can apply good pedagogy and a deep understanding of learning and development to the technologies of the moment. They will see opportunities and challenges for their learners and help navigate them, leveraging the affordances of the tools of the time.

Uncertain futures

The future of the workplace and the skills children will need to develop in order to thrive in an uncertain future are the subject of much discussion (Autor, Levy and Murnane, 2003). The most important point that consistently arises is that flexibility and adaptability will be vital. Thinking and problem-solving skills will come before technical ability on the presumption that it will be more important to be able to develop technical proficiency quickly with new tools than be an expert in something that may soon be obsolete.

The term 'digital literacy' is often encountered in contemporary discourse around technology and learning. The following section will explore this term, including its origins, and provide some opportunities to consider digital literacy skills.

Reflective questions

1. What digital skills do you have in the following areas?
    - Finding relevant digitally stored information,
    - choosing tools and platforms for different purposes,
    - recognizing the reliability of digital information and
    - choosing what you share and when.

2. What would you like to improve?
3. Which of these areas might children need help to become proficient with?
4. Why?
5. What form might that help take?

Literacy traditionally is associated with the skills of reading and writing. Comprehension may be considered to fall under that umbrella. A text can be defined as a 'motivated sign' (Kress and van Leeuwen, 2006, p. 154) or 'the realisation of a discourse in one or more semiotic modes' (Pahl, 2002, p. 146). There is an underlying human intention to encode an idea and make it accessible to another person either immediately or at another time or place. The earliest known record is a series of hand stencils in the Spanish cave of Maltraveiso, some of which are thought to be 64,000 years old (Hoffmann et al., 2018). Imagine a teenaged Palaeolithic hominid. They take a handful of coloured earth and place their palm on a cave wall, fingers spread, then blow the coloured dust onto the damp stone. What were they thinking and feeling? This was a motivated sign. The coloured earth and the damp wall were a technological innovation. That act, in motivation and emotional landscape, has commonalities with a young person uploading a video onto YouTube today.

The impact of advertising and digital media on adults and young people has long been discussed. Barthes (1972) highlights the nature of socially propagated mythologies and the willingness of the human mind to adopt a position because it is approved by a wider group. Being constantly exposed to the calculated intentions of advertisers and other internet users certainly brings with it risks. Recent research however (Orben, 2020) has found that although WHO (2019) recommendations suggest restricting screen time for young children and teenagers, there is currently no evidence of harm resulting from children and young people's typical media use. As educators, it is important to teach children to use media purposefully and to be critical consumers of the material they encounter.

Doug Belshaw developed a model he called the eight elements of digital literacy (2014). This model explores the role digital technologies have in different dimensions of modern life and the skills needed to make the most of the opportunities they offer.

These elements are:

1. *Cultural*: Belshaw stresses that this element is about the context in which a person is working while consuming or creating digital media.
2. *Cognitive*: This is about technical competencies with technologies. Such competencies are not normally goals themselves but rather necessary tools to be able to achieve other outcomes.

3. *Constructive*: This element of digital literacy focuses on recognizing the potential for different digital content, ideas and processes to be combined by, for example, remixing a video or adding sound to an animation using several different apps.

4. *Communicative*: Much of what is done with digital technologies is focused on communication. There are subtleties within this – on different platforms there are different sets of socially constructed rules. The networked nature of online communications requires a different mode of thought to face-to-face communication.

5. *Confident*: Belshaw frames this element in terms of resilience to new processes and willingness to explore new technology tools without becoming frustrated by new ways of working.

6. *Creative*: Technology has an endless potential to foster creative acts. Belshaw also notes that creativity is part of problem finding as well as problem solving.

7. *Critical*: This element links closely to what Barthes would have recognized as 'media literacy'. That is the ability to recognize the intentions of the authors of media viewed and to consider the intentionality behind one's own creative outputs.

8. *Civic*: Social movements are driven by the ability to engage with others and share ideas. There are constant examples in the mainstream media of large-scale movements driven by a connected public. There is also small-scale social activism happening that would not be possible without digital communications.

(Adapted from Belshaw, 2014, pp. 42–60)

Reflective questions

1. What digital literacy skills from Belshaw's eight elements do you use?
2. How did you learn these skills?
3. How do these skills fit into children's developmental progression?

Educators are now faced with classrooms where a fifth of children surveyed by NESTA identify as 'digital makers', that is as people who use digital technologies to create their own websites and apps; to modify games and remix media; even to control and create physical objects to share publicly or privately (Quinlan, 2015, p. 45).

Teachers have a responsibility to help learners develop the skills they need to capitalize on these interests and to ensure access to the opportunities to think in these new ways about the world in which they are growing up. They should be available to all children in a form that is developmentally and culturally appropriate and relevant.

Development with technology: What the research says

Lev Vygotsky said that 'what a child can do with assistance today, she will be able to do by herself tomorrow' (trans. 1978, p. 87). Technology can play a part in this in several ways:

1. as a way to access information to streamline learning experiences;
2. as a way to access pre-recorded skills-tutoring of more experienced human teachers through for example online videos;
3. as a way of engaging in dialogue with peers and mentors through online communities; and
4. as a way of consolidating learning through practice activities that give instant feedback.

Note that in all of these the technology simply mediates the engagement with Vygotsky's 'more knowledgeable other' (MKO) altering the location and time frame in which a learner can engage in dialogue with, and access materials created by, an MKO.

In this way, it is clear that technology can also facilitate scaffolding of learning in accordance with Bruner's (1966) modes of representation. Consider the Enactive; Iconic; Symbolic stages of learning: technology is particularly well suited to bridging the gaps between them. Having worked with manipulative resources for example, a learner can move on to manipulating representations of the same resources on a screen and gradually replace them with icons of the objects. Finally, those icons can be represented and manipulated on screen alongside the symbolic representations or with opportunities to switch quickly between one and the other allowing the learner to progress at a personalized pace through the levels of abstraction required to master the thinking skills involved.

Technology in the classroom and in everyday life can have an impact on many areas of development as follows:

Values: A person's values are socially constructed and when such a broad spectrum of experience is mediated by access to technology, individuals taking an interest in young children's development will benefit from an awareness of children's online activities and its influence on the values within the children's culture.

Spheres of influence: Bronfenbrenner's (1977) ecological model of development suggests that children's development is mediated by several levels of interpersonal engagement. Technology can shift these boundaries in a variety of ways:

- facilitating access to remote family members – for example, a parent in the forces – via video calling or groups chats;
- through the use of mobile apps to connect parents and teachers in real time so that dialogue between home-school life is more fluid; and
- by shaping connections with cultural role models via technology tools.

Cognitive: Cognitive skills such as analysis, design, decision making and problem solving are recognized as 'widely applicable' in real life (OECD, 2003). In one example, Akcaoglu and Koehler (2014) worked with middle-school-aged children learning computer game design. They found evidence supporting improved outcomes across these cognitive skills in their cohort. They also found that these skills were generalizable into other areas of learning.

Creative: McDougall (2013) used the term 'technology/creativity divide' to raise concerns about the separation of so-called creative subjects from other subjects that employ creative thinking – in particular, science and technology. He concluded that it is time for educators 'to decode the learning required for the twenty-first century by abandoning historical distinctions between creativity and technology' (p. 4).

Social and emotional well-being: As an emerging area of study, there is still 'a lack of clear cut evidence for a link between digital technology use and well-being' (Orben, 2020). OECD (2019) recommend that screen time is managed but does not suggest that it is harmful as part of a varied and healthy lifestyle. Two factors arise from these explorations: firstly, that screen time is an important part of the social fabric of children's worlds and secondly, that there is not yet any direct evidence of screen time as a causal factor for young people experiencing social and emotional problems.

Speech and language development: There is a growing body of evidence to justify the use of specialized technology-based tools to support children with speech and language delay (e.g. Cunningham, 2019; Du et al., 2019; Keighrey et al., 2017). Tate (2018) also found that prior technology exposure correlated with higher achievement in writing. There are gaps in the literature but there is a recognized potential for technology to have a positive role in exposing developing minds to a language-rich world. Heafner and Massey (2019, p. 455) for example explored technology-mediated learning of history-specific language noting 'the power and potential of online, mobile, and social media to promote the kind of rich and highly accessible word learning that has been previously beyond the reach of most students'.

Motor skills: The general conclusion in the literature is that digital technologies can complement non-technology-related activities in developing manual dexterity. They extend three-dimensional (3D) sensory experiences (Plowman et al., 2012; Payler et al., 2017) with, for example, opportunities to explore devices through different physical input methods, from mouse, to touch screen, to game controller. This diversifies opportunities for children to manipulate and explore the world around them. Savage and Barnett (2017, p. 76) also highlight the affordances of digital devices in supporting developmental aims, in particular the fact that such devices often have buttons, levers, switches and knobs that appeal to children's natural kinaesthetic exploratory urges.

So, it is clear that in this twenty-first-century age, the digital revolution is shaping many aspects of children's lives with their 'digital birth' taking place in the first trimester of pregnancy when those early scans are posted on social media. There is no escaping the fact technology will affect them in myriad ways from their birth onwards. Practitioners working with children owe it to them to reflect on the role the technology is playing in the environments they provide for the children and make sure that these experiences are positive and constructive.

Case study: What role does technology have in the British International School in Hanoi, Vietnam?

Country: Vietnam

Age group: Year 5

Setting: International School

Participants involved: Teacher and Year 5 pupils

Declan Barney qualified in 2012 in the UK, and after teaching the English National Curriculum in a small village school in Devon for two years, he took a post in the British International School in the Vietnamese city of Hanoi. The school is a prestigious fee-paying institution, and part of the Nord Anglia group.

Here is Mr Barney's perspective on the role technology has to play in the lives of the children he teaches and an example of a unit of work for those children that promotes the use of technology:

> When I think about the skills that my students will need as we move into a more digitalised and globalised world, there are two questions which I try to keep in mind; what do I want my students to be able to do that computers can't? And what context am I preparing my students to work in?
>
>   Computers are good at solving problems when they have all of the information that they need, and they know what the solutions are supposed to look like. Humans are much better at solving problems when we have no idea how to solve the problem, and no idea what the output is supposed to look like. In a world where jobs are increasingly

becoming automated, and even seemingly complex tasks are being reduced to an algorithm, it is essential that my students have skills at their disposal which cannot be reduced to a routine 'if-then-do' statement.

The particular context that I must prepare my students for is one where they may not be living or working in their home country of Vietnam. The expectations from a variety of stakeholders in the school are that my students will get their degrees abroad and probably work abroad too, potentially between different countries. This requires us to focus on the idea of 'international mindedness' at our school, and has inspired me to create opportunities for children to collaborate remotely on projects which surround solving global problems.

This outline of a unit of work I planned and delivered recently focused on the development of these skills. My Year 5 students were given the challenge to make a persuasive video to try to generate change due to the problem of micro plastics in our oceans. The following is an overview of the activities they completed.

- The students individually made a short video explaining what their strengths are in different areas of ICT (Information and Communications Technology). Another school in Hanoi did the same, and the students selected small groups to work with based on these videos.
- Each group created a cross-school collaborative document where they recorded their research about micro plastics in our oceans and information about the different places around the world with the best recycling projects.
- The students worked their way through a Hyperdoc. This document is a self-guided document, which takes them through the process of making a persuasive video.
- The persuasive videos were then made, based on the information contained in their collaborative research task.
- Their videos were uploaded to the app Flipgrid that enabled opportunities for peer-assessment.

One of the most important aspects of this unit of work was the initial short video in which the students explained their own strengths. This task was created with the idea that students are increasingly likely to be interviewed remotely in the future. Alongside this, the students then worked with team members they had not yet met. In our increasingly globalised world, this is becoming more and more ordinary in the workplace.

The benefits of a Hyperdoc are well documented but in summary, it provides the scaffolding and the extension tasks required for students to self-differentiate their learning process. It works as a guide for the students to use allowing them opportunities to solve problems and make decisions and access resources and materials throughout the process of making the video. When the students began using it, they had no idea what their final video would be about or what it would look like, but after working through a series of phases within the Hyperdoc they had planned their videos and were ready to make them. However, in the real world, there will not always be a Hyperdoc to guide them through complex problem solving; it acts as a good framework in a move towards completing such activities without the guidance. As well as this, Hyperdocs allows for a non-linear style of learning; every child engaged with the document differently, accessing different resources and materials, and differentiating the learning process themselves by accessing the materials they thought they needed to make a better persuasive video. The result was motivated learners.

Ultimately, I believe activities such as this help to prepare my students with the skills they will need to succeed in the international spaces they occupy.

Declan's commentary demonstrates a strong focus on *values* as discussed above. He indicates that the thinking skills associated with successful technology use are recognized as important for children growing up in the globally mobile group of people who choose to send their children to this kind of school.

The unit of work demonstrates a high level of self-guided work on the part of the children, and this is facilitated by carefully prepared technology resources. Looking back at Belshaw's (2014) model of digital literacy, all of the elements he described are promoted through Mr Barney's unit of work. In particular, it is worth taking note of the use of formative assessment in the initial task where the learners self-identified their strengths and constructed work groups based on these.

Reflective questions

Consider Declan's unit of work:

1. What impact do you think the initial task explaining ICT strengths had on the learners?
2. How does it link to each of the eight elements of digital literacy described in this chapter?
3. What support would you ask for to deliver this in your setting?
4. How could you use resources available to you to introduce a similar project?

Case study: Use of a visualizer to support learning across the curriculum in a small school in England

Country: England

Age group: Six to seven years

Setting: Primary school

Participants involved: Teacher and pupils

Rebecca Smallshaw works in a school on the South coast of England having trained to as a primary teacher specializing in ICT in the classroom. Here she shares one innovation she has employed to make the most of the limited technology available in her setting:

> From the perspective of a Year 2 (age 6–7 years) teacher at a small, one form entry, coastal village school with limited technology available, a key tool is the visualiser. With many uses, it has been a huge success and is definitely a contributing factor to many planned lessons. It is used predominantly for modelling learning and assessing the children across a variety of activities.
>
> When giving the children a whole class input during the lesson, the visualiser is used to model the skill or activity that the children will be completing. This allows children to gain an understanding of exactly what they need to do and how they need to do it in a format that is visible to all. When used appropriately and planned for effectively, this strategy consistently increases child engagement and therefore understanding, as well as reducing preparation time.
>
> Once the key skill has been modelled and the class activity is underway, the visualiser is then used as a tool for assessment at different points throughout the lesson, both from an academic point of view and in terms of learning dispositions. Once the children have started to work on a task, activity or skill, different examples of children's work can be shown on the visualiser. The children can then unpick any misconceptions together, or recognise and share where they have done something well. This can then lead on to the children seeing where they are in terms of the success criteria for that lesson and what their next steps might be. This allows the children to take ownership of their successes within that lesson, developing an understanding of responsibility and reflection, something that is at the core of this school's ethos.

Rebecca's lessons take full advantage of the flexibility afforded by the visualizer. The potential for collaborative learning, the promotion of metacognition and pupil's ownership of their learning come through as strengths of this approach.

Taking mathematics learning as an example, the use of technology in this way can bridge gaps in between Bruner's (1966) three modes of representation discussed previously. Using a visualizer, a teacher can model the enactive stage easily and then images from this modelling can be captured and used for the iconic stage either on screen, or printed out or drawn by children. The step from iconic to symbolic can also be modelled in this way helping children to move from concrete thinking to abstract conceptualization as advocated by Clark-Wilson and Mostert (2016).

An alternative to a visualizer is the use of a tablet device connected to a screen-casting service. This can be used in a very similar way to a visualizer by simply enabling the tablet's camera. The portability and familiarity of tablet devices mean that they can easily be handed around in this kind of lesson adding a further sense of ownership and interactivity to the experience of the learners.

Reflective questions

Consider the use of visualizers to share live images to a screen at the front of the classroom:

1. How can this be helpful when teaching practical subjects?
2. What forms of feedback does it promote and how might children engage with this feedback?
3. What impact might it have on children with diverse learning needs?

Technology supporting learning in the Core subjects

Having explored the case studies and seen just two examples of effective classroom practice using technology, it is worth reflecting on the potential of classroom technology to support learning in different curricular areas.

English instruction in primary schools covers a considerable range of skills and knowledge. This includes spoken language; encoding and decoding a range of text types; understanding grammatical constructions; through to the sophisticated recognition of inference and bias in fiction and non-fiction texts.

Technology can present diverse opportunities for learners to be immersed in a language-rich environment. Indeed, touch screen devices are becoming ever more central to what it means to be literate and productive in contemporary society (Parry et al., 2016, pp. 111–12). From an early age, children engage readily with digital devices and the potential of this to improve learning outcomes is gaining ever-wider recognition. For example, Zipke (2017) found that pre-school children's word recognition scores were higher for those who engaged with digital versions of stories with a read-aloud function than those with paper versions of the same tale. The study went on to find that interactive stories with animated sections led to higher levels of comprehension when children worked independently than when they worked with a teacher.

Technology also offers myriad opportunities for writing stimuli that are relevant to children and engage them in producing responses that are part of their cultural landscape and have intrinsic value to the children as producers of these artefacts. As a bridge into this, collaborative writing on a class screen can be a powerful way to create a starting point for novice writers deepening the sense of shared ownership (McFarlane, 2014, p. 117). Technology can also provide opportunities to access meaningful audiences for children's writing. This can be through sharing work on blogs or posting book reviews online. One child I know of had an Amazon book review used as part of the blurb on a new edition of their favourite book!

Mathematics also provides the innovative teacher with numerous opportunities to employ technology tools to enhance learning. There are numerous mathematics games offering motivating, gamified consolidation activities that are considerably more engaging than completing lists of calculations on paper. These tools can also give instant feedback to pupils as well as recording scores for teachers to identify topics or concepts that need further teaching.

Technologies offer diverse methods of displaying and modelling mathematical concepts in ways suitable for children at different stages of development, as discussed above in response to case study two. In addition to this, the use of physical resources such as robots can help to develop mathematical thinking, concepts around shape, space and measure, and promote the use of mathematical language. This can often take place through what Campbell and Walsh termed 'play based digital learning' (2017, p. 10). Such play-based learning is open ended and exploratory but can be purposeful at the same time when mediated by objects with specific affordances.

Science is a subject that is founded on a process: asking questions and then engaging with the world to generate experiences that help to answer those questions and generate further, more refined questions. Technology can play a number of roles in this. First of all when making and documenting observations of natural phenomena, technology tools can help by capturing moments, magnifying and measuring objects and environments, and accessing a wider community of people doing similar science. Second is the area of science communication. There may well be children who are good at scientific thinking but struggle to complete written 'reports' about their science. Technology enables the creation of interactive presentations as alternative models of reflecting on scientific classroom activities. It can be used to record and collate a range of information using digital cameras, data loggers and digital microscopes; it also continually extends the possibilities for presenting and reporting ideas and findings (Harlen and Qualter, 2018, p. 263; Qualter, 2011, pp. 66–7), thus enabling a broad spectrum of children to make progress in their science learning. This immediate record and the ease with which it can be shared is also a powerful tool for helping children recognize and unpack misconceptions they may have, through dialogue and metacognition.

Technology as a curriculum subject

Most of the discussions thus far in this chapter have focused on technology as a tool for learning. It is important to be aware of the difference between this and technology as a subject in its own right. In the English National Curriculum, *Computing* is recognized as a distinctive programme of study (DfE, 2013).

The statements in the computing curriculum are separated by Key Stage (KS), with the KS1 (Key Stage 1: Years 1 and 2, ages five to seven) objectives being reflected in KS2 (Key Stage 2: Years, 3, 4, 5 and 6, ages seven to eleven) but with a higher level of sophistication. The statements can be divided up under three headings as follows:

1. *Computer science.* This is recognized as the programming or coding dimension of technology use. It can be thought of as understanding how computers work. It involves writing and editing simple programs to, for example, control a character on a screen or to program a simple robot to solve a maze. The terms 'Algorithm', 'debug' and 'computational thinking' are central to this area of learning.
2. *Information technology.* This involves children learning to use everyday technology tools to create, share and access digital artefacts. It extends from basic skills like mouse use and saving and retrieving files, to creating and editing video and animations or publishing their creations on suitable online platforms.
3. *Digital literacy.* This can be thought of as the human dimension of technology use. It includes understanding the ways in which we interact via technology-mediated channels. It also encompasses the serious topic of online safety. Within this, learning to be critical consumers of digital media is another important area of learning.

Teachers may believe that children are more capable than them with technology, viewing young people as digital residents and seeing themselves as digital visitors (White and LeCornu, 2011). This binary view is rarely the case. Children may be proficient at particular games or at using online video platforms, but they may never have used a desktop PC or created a digital object themselves. Responsible educators will look at these skills and ensure that they are given dedicated teaching time rather than assuming children will pick them up along the way. As teachers of the computing curriculum, do not expect to have all the answers. A willingness to explore, to make mistakes and to model how to learn from them has the potential to be wonderfully inspiring for the digital trail blazers of the future.

Indeed, teacher confidence is one of the biggest barriers to effective technology-based learning; however, this can be countered by teacher's self-belief and the resultant self-efficacy in technology integration (Kwon et al., 2019). This creates a cultural capital around technology use and leads to wider adoption of related practices across the learning community. Investment in three areas is key to achieving this. Reliable and up-to-date equipment is the first. Second is suitable access to technical support. Third and most important is suitable training in the relevant technology tools. Budgeting for investment in any new equipment must include opportunities for staff members to learn to use it and provide opportunities for them to share their practice so it becomes self-sustaining.

Conclusion

Technology is percolating through into more and more elements of modern life. The lives of the children educators work with will be ever more deeply infused with the riches and challenges this brings.

Those working with children in any setting have a threefold responsibility: firstly, to recognize and respect the role that digital technology plays in the lives of the young people they work with; secondly, to leverage the potential of the technologies available to provide rich and relevant experiences for the children in their settings; and thirdly, to teach children the skills and knowledge they need to thrive in a technology rich society.

To do this successfully an awareness of Doug Belshaw's eight elements of digital literacy will serve as a good framework for reflection, for professional development and for curriculum planning. If teachers model the attitudes associated with these twenty-first-century literacies, children will adopt them and be ready for their future – a future no one has yet imagined.

Reflective questions

As a professional how do you engage with the core themes of this chapter?

1. Technology is a tool for all aspects of pedagogy.
2. Teachers have a responsibility to adopt technology into their teaching in order to reflect the lives of the children that they work with.
3. Technology offers new insights into theories (and models) of learning.

> ## Reflexive question
>
> As a professional how do you engage with these core themes in relation to your own emotions and assumptions and biases?

Annotated bibliography

Orben, A. (2020). 'Teenagers, screens and social media: A narrative review of reviews and key studies'. *Social Psychiatry and Psychiatric Epidemiology*, **55, pp. 407–14.**

This paper helpfully reviews a wide range of evidence on the effect of digital technology on the psychological well-being of adolescents. While highlighting issues with the quality of some of the research available, the conclusions broadly indicate that the effect of digital technology on psychological well-being is on average negative, but very small, with uncertainty about the direction of the links between the two.

Quinlan, O. (2015). *Young digital makers.* **London: Nesta.**

This report looks at the opportunities for young people to create using digital technology. Drawing on survey data the report looks at young people's and parents' broadly positive views on digital making, while highlighting that often teachers can lack in confidence in teaching the ICT curriculum.

6

Listening to Children

Cheryl Graham and Verity Campbell-Barr

Introduction

The area of interest for this chapter is adult interactions with two- to four-year-old children in an early years setting with a focus on concepts of 'listening'. Having set the context for early years education, we consider how policy, early years pedagogy and society have constructed perspectives on listening to children, and how concepts of listening have been developed to engage with children's views and interests, to inform practice in early years settings. The aim of this chapter is to support those who work with young children to develop an awareness of what listening constitutes and how to engage with, and interpret, guidelines and a curriculum that appear to impose particular meaning onto the concept of listening. We advocate and discuss a holistic approach to 'tune in' (Trevarthen, 2013) to children and the long-term benefits of creating a 'culture of listening' (Robinson and Aronica, 2014). Whilst the focus of the chapter is on early years education, the debates considered will raise pertinent questions as to whether those working with children of different ages really 'listen'.

A brief context

To give a context for the topic of listening to children it is useful to consider socio-cultural influences that have shaped our view of childhood and concepts of listening to children. One significant factor (in the UK) was the introduction of education in 1880 for all children aged between five and ten years old. The introduction of compulsory schooling led to the study of child development (Hendrick, 1997, p. 47), whereby mass schooling allowed for children to become 'research-subjects', opening public debate on the physical and mental health of children and the value of education for children. Child study was viewed as being able to understand and provide solutions to the social, economic and political problems of the day; it supported the new social and political identity of children as becoming citizens of tomorrow. Children were 'reconstructed as material investments in national progress' (Hendrick, 1997, p. 51), something that resonates in modern conceptions of education.

Over the years, the process of 'schooling' has filtered below children aged five and started to include what is now known as the early years. The early years sector provides learning development and care for children from birth to five years and includes childminders, daycare, pre-schools and reception classes in schools (Campbell-Barr, 2015). A comprehensive history of early years education for pre-school children is not within the scope of this chapter. However, it is recognized that the framework for the Early Years Foundation Stage (EYFS) and the development of Ofsted inspections (in England), centralized regulation and national standards, which have been constructed over the past two decades, have shaped early years practice (Hevey, 2012; Lloyd, 2014; Moss, 2014a) and have consequences for the concept of listening to children.

Government initiatives and early years interventions suggest that given defined programmes, children will progress developmentally. We do not dispute the importance of early years education in supporting the holistic development of young children, but our concern lies with whether restricted and narrowly defined concepts of child development have had consequences for concepts of listening within the early years. Working practice has been directed and influenced within England (and other parts of the UK) by Government initiatives and the development of different and occasionally conflicting advice or approaches to supporting children's development. Some has been very positive, as recognition is given to the importance of children's learning and development in the early years, with a valuing of their life experiences as indicated in the EYFS (Department for Education, 2014). However, there is a question as to whether introducing centralized regulations and national standards has implications for professional practice. In particular, we are interested in whether centralized regulation imposes a narrow adult agenda onto the concept of listening.

Theoretical framework

Human Capital Theory stresses the value of education to individuals and society as key to the economy (Heckman, 2000). Investments in early years education have been presented as offering higher economic returns than investments in any other stage of education. However, as Penn (2012) argues, the Human Capital approach does not allow for inequities and makes an assumption of agreed inputs with expected outputs as to the role and purpose of early years services. Globally, Human Capital Theory has proved persuasive among policymakers, but it is a model that focuses on the becoming child, rather than one that values the child and listening to them in the here and now (Campbell-Barr and Leeson, 2016).

Moss (2014b, p. 19) refers to Human Capital Theory as a 'story of quality and high returns' and introduces Foucault's idea that areas of social life are influenced by powerful discourses. The discourse of quality and high returns represents a dominant, taken-for-granted view of early years services as producing economic returns for children (on their entering adulthood), families and society. However, the determining of quality and economic value presupposes a set of outcomes to be achieved. The early years settings that best meet the outcomes are those that will be judged to be of the highest quality and offering the best value. However, the appropriation of a social discourse for political means results in some outcomes being valued over others, distorting the concept of quality. The emphasis on particular outcomes will impact on the adult/child relationship and the ways in which adults listen to children. Pertinent to our discussion is whether a focus on outcomes results in a limited concept of listening.

The EYFS (Department for Education, 2014) suggests expected outcomes for children and through a process of standardization, the Government measures, quality-assures and evaluates children's learning and development in the early years. The question arises as to whether a focus on frameworks to measure and make judgements on the working practice of adults affects the way adults hear children's voices.

As an example, the area of *Positive Relationships* in the EYFS highlights that trusting relationships are formed by listening to children, giving consideration to different needs such as English as an additional language. *Creativity and Critical* thinking is an aspect of *Learning and Development* and an approach which is promoted in the EYFS as Sustained Shared Thinking (SST). SST is

> *an episode in which two or more individuals work together in an intellectual way to solve a problem, clarify a concept, evaluate activities, extend a narrative etc. Both parties must contribute to the thinking and it must develop and extend.*
>
> Siraj-Blatchford et al. (2002, p. 8)

The premise of SST is to provide opportunities for adults to support children's ideas and help children to have authenticity and become self-regulated learners. However, the approach also indicates an underlying adult agenda by including open-ended questions to prompt responses and gain information. While we do not dispute that those working in the early years will be motivated by wanting to support and extend children's development, we question whether the good intentions of SST become distorted when placed within a model whereby children and the early years settings that they attend are assessed based upon their performance of, and in, the EYFS.

All early years settings and Ofsted registered providers must follow the EYFS. Through an inspection process, settings will be judged on their quality. The judgement is, in part, about their adherence to the EYFS, but it is also about how well children are supported in their developmental outcomes. The inspection process introduces penalties through a grading system and funding can be removed from a failing setting according to their inspection criteria (Campbell-Barr and Leeson, 2016). Although there has to be some system of accountability in a publicly funded system, we would argue that learning is not 'an industrial process … it is an organic one' and that 'the problem with conformity in education is that people are not standardised to begin with' (Robinson and Aronica, 2014, p. 36). Thus, the assessment of the settings and the children is against some mythical norm, where failure to conform can result in negative labels. The consequences of such an inspection system will distort the ways in which professionals listen to children.

Window on practice

New Zealand – A case study of a curriculum for listening

Te Whāriki is the New Zealand early childhood curriculum. It was first introduced in 1996 and updated in 2017. The curriculum is underpinned by a view of children as capable and confident learners, with an emphasis on hearing and listening 'to the passionate spirit of the child' (Lee, 2015). Te Whāriki is not bound by developmental milestones, but instead adopts a holistic view of children's development and the knowledge, skills, attitudes and learning dispositions needed to be robust and resilient learners in the school system. The curriculum puts the child at the centre, with an expectation that educators will respond to the capabilities and contexts of the children attending their early years service. Educators use learning stories as a way of presenting the narratives of children's learning to document children's progress. The stories focus on children's successes and can provide a way to communicate with parents and reflect on practice, often adopting visual as well as written documentation.

Dahlberg et al. (2013) suggest that the process rather than the outcomes should be valued in assessments of quality and that the relationship between the adult and child needs to be recognized, even if it cannot always be measured. Modernist approaches of scientific rationality favour models of quality with observable and measurable features. Conversely, Dahlberg and Moss (2005) offer the notion of an ethic of care, which focuses on the relational and inter-subjective, recognizing the moral responsibility for the other. The pedagogical relationship and the importance of co-construction in the relationship need to be recognized in assessments of quality, even if it cannot be measured. Focusing on the pedagogical relationship presents a different framework for the concept of listening.

Co-construction recognizes the child as a social actor, valuing the child as having agency, which impacts on the relationship between the adult and the child. Viewing the child in this way requires the adult to listen to the child and gain the child's perspective. In listening, the adult helps the child to actively think about their experiences and learning, thus both valuing the being child, while supporting them in actively becoming (Lee, 2003).

To develop a culture of listening and learning how to listen, Davies (2014, p. 34) argues, is being open to being affected and the possibility of change rather than fitting into what we already know. She uses the term 'listening-as-usual' where existing categories are used to constantly make judgements of the individual and creates an identity for both the listener and the listened to. Her suggestion is that this creates a fear of not being good enough as each individual attempts to live up to an ideal. She argues that this is exacerbated by the neo-liberal approach which dominates educational institutions in the UK which promotes individualism by encouraging competition at school and work. This echoes the model of quality and high returns referred to earlier (Moss, 2014b). However, Davies offers a model of listening not as judgement of categorical difference but as valuing difference and is more than decoding sound for meaning, but requires whole attention and orientation and a 'suspension of our judgements and above all our prejudices' (Rinaldi quoted in Davies, 2014, p. 21). She emphasizes the importance of remaining open to the 'not-yet-known' through the process of emergent listening.

Window on practice

Cheryl's encounter with valued listening

An adult and three children were playing a new game that the adult had introduced. There were frog bean bags in four different colours and circle mats in matching colours. The children were encouraged to throw the frogs on to the matching mat.

Another child came over and took the green frog and mat away from the group. Adults responded by encouraging the child to join in the game and take turns. The child didn't want to, becoming very distressed and running to another part of the garden. I went over to the child and sat beside them quietly, by way of inviting them to tell me all about what was happening. I did not ask any questions or talk to them, but gave them time to respond to me; after about thirty seconds (it felt long at the time) the child said: 'I just want to hold these forever.'

I knew green was the child's favourite colour from previous observations, and so I nodded, then repeated the comment 'you just want to hold them' and added 'you do like green'. We sat together in silence for two minutes while the child hugged the toys, then they got up, gave the toys back and went off to play.

> When the child said, 'I want to hold these forever', looking through the child's eyes to understand, I thought of my two very grown-up sons, and when we meet we always hug and 'I want to hold them forever'. Forever is not possible, but a minute or two along the way is treasured. When the child gave the toys back, a member of staff asked what I had said to the child, and I replied 'I listened'.

In this example, the child had been listened to, which was a need that had been satisfied and so enabled him to return the items. 'It's not about outward appearances, but inward significance' (Tartt, 2013, p. 853). However, the context was 'being listened to' as opposed to 'being directed'. By developing a pedagogy where aspects such as self-esteem, confidence and respect are valued and considered a priority, we are trusting and respecting children as beings in their own right.

Reflective question

How do we allow for time, not only for us to tune in to children but also to allow the children to tune into us, to develop a dynamic and trusting relationship. What might be the differences when working with more vulnerable children with behavioural and attachment difficulties?

Theories of listening

Reggio Emilia is an educational philosophy based on the image of the child. It was established in the Municipal Infant-toddler Centres and the Preschools of Reggio Emilia, Italy. Loris Malaguzzi (Malaguzzi, 1994), founder of the Reggio Emilia Approach, refers to the diverse ways in which children communicate in his poem 'The Hundred Languages of Children'. Reference is made to the varied ways that children explore, make connections and communicate their experiences, which implies that there are diverse ways for adults to tune into and listen to children. The approach is 'project based' and incorporates children's ideas, indicating a strong desire to value and listen to the children. Stewart (2011, p. 12) suggests that Reggio Emilia is reflected in children's playing and exploring when 'children are engaged as agents in their own learning', as she explains that although what children learn is important so is how they learn.

It is important to recognize that the Reggio Approach derived from the social conditions in which it developed. Therefore, transferring the ideas and ethos of the Approach to different contexts risks diluting or distorting its original meaning. Furthermore, there is a risk that it imposes a particular set of expectations onto children, whereby they have the necessary cultural capital to express themselves and articulate their learning (Dahlberg et al., 2013). Arguably, the Approach still maintains expectations of what children should be able to do – all-be-it with less prescriptive outcomes than discussed earlier. However, the core ideology that children communicate in different ways implies that those working with children will need to listen in different ways.

Reflective questions

1. How do our own cultural influences impact our behaviour and attitudes towards listening to children?
2. What might be the implications for children?

Nyland et al. (2008) support the diverse ways that children communicate by recognizing that gesture conveys meaning differently from speech. Gestures are a natural way of communication for young children and can convey information and insight as they develop language. They concluded that through the medium of the language of hands, adults can observe and interpret children's thinking and learning. Recognizing the significance of gesture can present opportunities to develop shared understandings and to 'listen' to children's responses and intentional communications. This supports the idea that listening to children is a process that is not limited to the spoken word and the potential for children to express themselves in non-verbal ways. Children can transmit their ideas, views and experiences through actions and reactions, whereby the voices of young children begin at birth (Clark and Moss, 2011).

Trevarthen (2013) considers the importance of listening and 'tuning in' as an integral element of interaction. He recognizes that communication with children is important from when they are babies and is embedded in how we care for them. Before a child has language, response by a caring adult is prompted by sound and gesture which leads to a 'conversational exchange'. Trevarthen (2013) has researched the development of language and relationships with babies and carers. His research on the rhythm and musicality of interactions between adults and babies, although focusing on the babies' development, enables us to reflect on how, even at the formative age of around five months, the melodic patterns develop in an intuitive way to build a relationship, encourage communication and develop an understanding. His research identified the significance of the note of middle C in pre-verbal interactions where the adult is literally 'tuning-in' to the infant. For babies to have their needs met they need a caring adult who listens to them and can interpret and tune in to their communication. How we listen to children can impact on their responses in later life. Trevarthen (2013) suggests that what children perceive and learn is influenced by what they do and on self-created agency. Knowing anything together with feeling must be a two-way process which is shared, including impulses, feelings and body movement. Again it is the emphasis on shared understanding rather than the adult interpretation to fit what is heard to what we already know.

Athey (2009) was working towards a constructivist pedagogy and was interested in the processes by which children construct their own knowledge. Athey's (2009, p. 50) interest in what children were doing revealed patterns of repeated behaviours 'into which experiences are assimilated and are gradually co-ordinated'. Her research encourages an affirmative approach, what are children doing, rather than a deficit model of a checklist which indicates what children are not doing or for planning next steps in children's learning.

There is a risk that quiet children can go unheard, but in focusing on the non-verbal, such as repeated actions, adults can listen and begin to know the child, whereby knowledge is conceptualized as broad and varied (Campbell-Barr, 2019). Arnold (2010) recognized that some schema indicated a representation of children's emotional worlds. *Young children seem to use schemas or repeated patterns of action for comfort, to form to, and to explore and begin to understand complex life events and changes* (Arnold, 2010, p. 11). Arnold proposes that understanding schema in children's play supports adults' understandings of children; repeated actions enable children to internalize, reflect on experiences and also anticipate future events. The value of understanding children supports their well-being and builds resilience to help them to feel secure.

Theories of listening draw attention to the multiple ways that children communicate, especially in non-verbal ways. While careful attunement to the child can support adults in listening to children's different forms of communication (Georgeson, 2018), there are research tools and curriculum approaches that can facilitate listening.

Listening in practice

The Mosaic Approach is a multi-method research approach that draws on the sociology of childhood in adopting the construct of the child as an active learner. Developed for working with three and four year olds it has been adapted for working with younger children and those for whom English is an additional language (Clark and Moss, 2011, p. 2). The aim of the Approach is to recognize children's competencies and develop early years services that are responsive to the voice of the child. The Approach adopts participatory methods including observations, child conferencing, child tours, child mapping, role play and gaining the perspectives of practitioners, parents and researcher(s) (Clark and Moss, 2011). The different participatory techniques were introduced to provide a variety of ways to listen to the child. Furthermore, the multiple method approach acknowledged how observations alone would provide an adult perspective.

The approach is identified as respectful not only of children's views, but also of their silences. Cameras were introduced to support the tours and map making so that children could photograph their favourite places and review and revisit them using the images. The approach is viewed as a way of listening to young children by using both verbal and visual information as a method of consultation and acknowledging the child and the adult as co-constructors of meaning.

However, Palaiologou (2014) questions whether we hear what children say and considers the ethical praxis when choosing research tools with children under five. The suggestion is that the issue of young children as participants in research is complex and requires continuous and critical reflection as the term 'participation' may provide an illusion of consent and consultation (Mohan, 2001). Palaiologou (2014) argues that consent through participation can be viewed as a top-down and adult led approach to ethical practice, which does not address the asymmetric power relations of children with adults.

Friere's (1996) theory of praxis refers to informed action by combining abstract theory and concrete action, where experience can shape our understanding of theory. Palaiologou (2014) uses the term 'ethical praxis' to highlight that participation of young children in research has complexities of ethics and there is a need to focus on child–adult relationships and create ethical spaces for children within the research process. The relevance of the relationship of the child and adult needs to be highlighted as it is integral to listening to and hearing children. Although the Mosaic Approach views the child and the adult as co-constructors of meaning, Palaiologou emphasizes that the *relationship* should be the focus rather than the method to ensure we hear the child. As concepts and methods become embedded, there is the potential to develop a linear conception of children's voices with an adult agenda. An open-ended question is still a question and if adults are asking questions are they really listening if they do not recognize that listening to children needs to be 'grounded in the asymmetric power relations between children and adults' (Palaiologou, 2014, p. 6).

To recognize the agency of the child is to understand how their level of well-being will influence their receptive state and offers a holistic approach to observing and listening to children. Laevers et al. (2012) suggest that by observing children's well-being and involvement, the focus is on how children experience and thrive in the environment provided for them, rather than 'traditional monitoring systems that tend to focus on academic achievements' (Laevers et al., 2012, p. 6). He developed a scale as a guide for measuring well-being and involvement, and the approach provides a lens for observing children's personal, social and emotional development. His approach includes the interactions of the child in relation to family members, other children and adults and their environment. Although this could still fit with an adult agenda of observing rather than listening to children, it does move towards recognizing the significance of children's emotional involvement.

Both the Mosaic Approach and Laevers observation tools provide mechanisms with which educators can explore different ways of listening to children, although both indicate cautionary notes about the dominance of adult agendas in framing how children are heard. However, there is also something to be said for the environment in which listening takes place. A study by Murray and O'Brien (cited in Tovey, 2007) suggests that practitioners gained new perspectives and understanding from observing children in a different environment. Forest School is presented as creating a culture of listening, leading to closer and more trusting relationships between the children and the adults (see Chapter 4). The ethos of Forest School builds on innate motivation and a positive attitude to learning, as well as promotes independence, opportunities to take risks, make choices and develop self-esteem and confidence (Doyle, 2006, cited in Tovey, 2007). This promotes the view of children as competent, capable, curious, adventurous and imaginative and suggests the possibility to transfer the ethos into other environments. It also illustrates that different environments will offer different opportunities for listening as children encounter multiple opportunities to express themselves.

Tovey (2007) does critique the UK interpretation of the Danish Forest School approach and ethos. She suggests that the UK curriculum lends the potential for didactic lessons where the children are not to wander out of sight. There is, therefore, the suggestion that adults become watchers and observers rather than listening to and engaging with the different actions and emotions of the children. The cautionary tale is again about educators opening themselves up to possibilities, rather than fitting into what is already known in order to adopt an ethos of listening.

Window on research

Graham, C. (2016). *Do concepts of listening to children mean we really hear their voice?* MA Dissertation submitted to the University of Plymouth.

Given my interest in the concept of listening, I looked to explore what listening meant within my own pre-school. I undertook

- interviews to ask participants about their meaning of 'listening',
- observations of how adults listen to children and
- follow-up interviews with participants to reflect on the observations.

The design of the research was to encourage individual interpretations, narratives and experiences. There were five participants for the project. They had a range of experience, background and qualifications in the early years sector and were all working with pre-school children in an early years setting. This diversity supported the data collection with narratives of individual voices being reflected in the analysis. Narrative analysis considers how people make meaning of their experiences and how they interpret them (Rubin and Rubin, 2012).

There were five categories that emerged from the data:

I. participants' view of their role and rationale for observing/listening to children,

II. participants' reflections on how to observe/listen to children,

III. participants' specific references to listening to children,

IV. external pressures/guidance that influences working practice and

V. perceived constraints/barriers to observing/listening to children.

Initial analysis indicated that external guidance had an impact on working practice with regard to observing and listening to children. There was a strong emphasis on the role of the adult to engage with children to assess or make judgements in order to encourage and identify progress. The EYFS document was highlighted most often.

Participants initially interpreted 'listening to children' literally with a shared understanding that 'good' or 'effective' listening meant being in a quiet space with a small group or 1:1 giving the children undivided and uninterrupted attention. Influences on listening included the environment, previous experiences (such as being a parent or previous working roles), their own childhoods and working with colleagues.

During the enquiry, there was a shift towards a more holistic view of the child. Participants reflected on observing children to notice their emotional resilience, well-being, how children responded differently to different adults and the value of building a picture of the child. Through a negotiation exercise the rationale for listening became 'tuning in' and 'building relationships'.

Using a multi-method approach to listen to children (Clark and Moss, 2011) developed participants' confidence to use both verbal and visual information, to stand back and observe behaviours to inform their understanding of the children – hearing the child's voice by gaining a perspective through the child's view.

Reducing the pressure of an adult agenda to 'tick boxes' and 'fill gaps' transforms the adult's role. Observing, listening, understanding and hearing children become more holistic and reflect the needs of the child now and build solid foundations rather than 'rushing children to a next stage' (Nutbrown and Clough, 2014, p. 80).

This project was not to apportion blame to Government or policymakers, however the influence of the EYFS in shaping an approach to listening in early years practice cannot be dismissed. However, the research project did encourage discussion of alternative frameworks which could provide a more holistic approach to working practice. By considering alternative approaches and theories, the staff in the pre-school explored the values of the setting and what they meant by listening. The culture of a setting is shaped by interpretations of the curriculum, assessment practices and pedagogical values. To challenge and interpret the curriculum to shape working practice for the benefit of the children requires confidence and knowledge of young children's play and learning. The focus for change was framed by how we observe and listen to children in our day-to-day practice and the benefits of listening to children in the early years, and creating a culture where children's voices are heard. Listening in the pre-school became removed from the EYFS and became central to our values.

Conclusion

How educators observe and listen to children in day-to-day practice will impact on their relationships with children. Hearing the child's voice is more than listening to their speech and language, but developing the skill of tuning in to their behaviour and understanding their communication with a holistic approach (Goldschmied and Jackson, 1994 cited in Clark and Moss, 2011) as children's behaviours can reflect their internal dialogues of experience and their emotional well-being (Laevers et al., 2012).

The benefits of listening to children in the early years develop trusting and secure relationships, and influence self-esteem and well-being, and are in contrast to a working practice which is contained within a standardized framework of assessment and outcomes. Where children know they are heard, trusting and secure relationships can be developed which in turn support their self-esteem and well-being and this can have an impact on their responses and resilience in later life.

As educators reflect on their pedagogical values and working practice, they should explore strategies to support active listening and recognize the benefits of meaningful listening where the child not only has the right to be heard but also that listening is central to teaching and learning (Podmore et al., 2001).

Reflective questions

As a professional how do you engage with the core themes of this chapter:

1. children as actively becoming,
2. regulations and curricula can confine how we listen to children and
3. listening is about more than verbal sounds and utterances.

> ## Reflexive question
> As a professional how do you engage with these core themes in relation to your own emotions and assumptions and biases?

Annotated bibliography

Friere, P. (1996). *Pedagogy of the oppressed*. London: Penguin.
Friere is considered a key part of the critical pedagogy movement. This text is seen as one of the seminal texts in the critical pedagogy movement and still resonates with readers over fifty years after it was first published. The book is celebrated for challenging the notion that learners are like empty vessels to be filled with knowledge, instead advocating learners as co-creators of knowledge.

Malaguzzi, L. (1993). *Your image of the child: Where teaching begins*, Unknown, Reggio Emilia.
The work of Malaguzzi is celebrated in early childhood education and care circles for highlighting how children communicate in multiple ways – referred to as the 100 Languages. He also encouraged educators to think about their image of the child and how it impacts on their interactions with the child – and how they listen to them. Malaguzzi encourages educators to think about whether their image of the child is the same as the child who stands before them and to consider how that might shape the relationship between the child and the educator.

7

Professional Relationships and Collaboration

Jessica Johnson and Norma Goodyear

'Knowing that N works in the school my girls attend, and that she gets them and me, is amazing.'

Mother (Case Study C)

Why include a chapter on professional relationships in a book on Child Development? While other chapters may cover knowledge of child development in regard to individuals and groups, sound relational pedagogy (Loe, 2014, Reeves and Le Mare, 2017) throughout daily practice has the potential to enhance and enrich the teaching and learning environment for all. Relationships embrace daily practice. No one works in isolation. Pupils, families, peers, colleagues and other professionals provide opportunities to develop collaborative relationships that may be modelled through varied and complex levels of communication and engagement. Pupils may continually observe a reflective teacher, who is willing to acknowledge personal, social and emotional responsibility for modelling, building and sustaining collaborative relationships (Vangrieken et al., 2017), enhancing holistic child development. This chapter is organized around a selection of case studies that provide you with opportunities to explore those complex relationships and collaborations – coming to better know yourself and the communities with whom you work and within which you practice.

Know yourself

'Learning to relate to others is where a person's sense of identity and belonging begins' (Loe, 2014, p. 1). Consider the energy used daily to sustain and build professional relationships – each pupil, staff member, parent, teacher and other professional. This is an offering of 'self' in both relational giving and receiving. How is it that some relationships may energize, some may be draining and others may pass unnoticed? Bourdieu (1992) acknowledges how 'social' and 'cultural capital' built up through individual past experiences with others can lead to unique ways of relating to and learning from others in different environments. Consider how this may be represented in the following case study A.

Case study A: Newly qualified teacher, peer observations and mentoring

Country: England

Age group: Adult

Setting: Primary school (five to eleven years)

Participants involved: Newly qualified teacher (NQT), teacher mentor

Before starting the School Direct programme (DfE, 2018a), the idea of being observed filled me with dread. Coming from an industry outside of education, the concept of it was completely alien to me and, through the sheer panic, I couldn't see the benefit of colleagues coming into your classroom to 'judge' you. Now, having completed my training, my fear of observations has been redressed and, not only that, I fully embrace them and, dare I say it, enjoy them. In the fast pace of the classroom environment, where it is easy to feel bogged down with the infinite extras you could be doing to support each child in your class, they are an opportunity to receive positive feedback on how well you are challenging and progressing your pupils, as well as being given constructive points of development and practical suggestions on implementation. Equally, I found that being afforded the opportunity to go into other classrooms was absolutely fundamental to my training; giving me a valuable insight into varieties of classroom management, behaviour management and application of pedagogical theories, which informed my own practice and helped me to knit together my teaching style. Attending lectures and in-school training sessions formed the backbone of the course and provided a wealth of theoretical information that, at times, felt overwhelming. In order to take this information and make it applicable to my own classroom setting, my mentor, who was also the class teacher, advised that I should aim to take away three key points from each session; one strategy that I could implement in class the following day and another two that I could introduce at a later date with the whole class or specific pupils. After each training session, I would discuss these points with my mentor and between us we would agree a way in which I could fit them into my lessons.

Outcomes Peer observations and constructive focused mentoring (Beek, Zuiker and Zwart, 2018) provide informed, reflective opportunities to increase self-awareness, celebrate professional development and achievement and create strategies that enhance teaching and learning. Within this 'new' context, social, cultural and professional capitals are being enriched (Hargreaves and Fullan, 2013).

What we can learn As Anna Richards, the Executive Leader of Suffolk and Norfolk SCITT comments, 'We know at heart that relationships influence the ways in which people cope with stress, access support and advice, learn, collaborate, and find fulfilment in their work' (Relationships Foundation, 2019, webpage).

The independent nature of teaching is evident in the case study, along with a willingness to benefit from Continuing Professional Development (CPD) with others (Eraut, 2007). A teacher continues to absorb new knowledge and experiences throughout daily practice. Autonomy is valued, yet also enhanced within a collaborative, interdependent climate (Vangrieken et al., 2017, p. 313) and with specific mentoring skills (Beek, Zuiker and Zwart, 2018). Teachers need to come to know themselves through the professional collaborative relationships that they form.

Reflective questions

1. Can you recollect your training?
2. Who was influential in guiding your practice?

Reflexive questions

1. Why was this person (or persons) influential in guiding your practice?
2. How did they make you feel?

Know your 'unique' communities

'If you want to lead people, you have to enter their world' (Bennis in Garelli, 2017, p. 1). Child Development may be visualized within an ecological model (Bronfenbrenner, 1979; Music, 2017, p. 269). Bronfenbrenner's 'Ecological Systems Theory' highlights the environmental impact on individual and group development, framing these influences within micro-systems, meso-systems, exo-systems and macro-systems and acknowledging change over time, the chrono-system. The micro-system represents relationships closest to the child within everyday life including each setting where the individual is an active participant such as family, friends, children's centre, nursery pre-school and school. Professional relationships may link outside the classroom and school, bridging other micro-systems within a meso-system: home within the local community, faith communities and health and social care provision. Teachers may consider how interaction with changing community resources may benefit the pupils in their class and/or school. Consider, in case study B, how the reflective practitioner's knowledge and skills increased specific community awareness for the benefit of children's learning and development.

Case study B: Children's Centre Manager and the local military barracks

Country: England

Age group: Adults

Setting: Children's Centre

Participants involved: Children's centre manager and seven mothers from a local military barracks

The locality of my children's centre and school encompasses a military barracks. This barracks is unique because it houses families from all three of the UK armed forces, known as tri-service accommodation. It is usual for the barracks to be occupied by one regiment made up of a wide range of military disciplines in order for them to carry out a variety of military tasks. Living in a regimental barracks means that all the serving partners will be deployed at the same time, resulting in the spouses/partners that are left behind providing a support network for each other should difficulties arise during the term of deployment. Until two years ago many of the families that resided in this accommodation were families of senior ranking officers whose children attended boarding school. However, this has recently changed and the barracks has now become home to lower-ranking personnel, many of whom have young families who attend the local children's centre and school. Five out of seven mothers within my small research study stated that the infrastructure within the barracks did not offer sufficient support to manage everyday life should their partner be deployed. They felt they were offered very little support compared to other barracks. References to support included lack of activities for families, no central meeting point and the barracks not being family-orientated. One person stated, 'Rank gets in the way of us supporting each other.' A selection of responses received generated common concerns:

'Living in this accommodation I can sometimes feel isolated because there isn't a community.'

'It can be lonely without the work contacts of our partners.'

Outcomes The building of effective support networks for this diverse group of tri-service families is more challenging as this unique group do not share a common military support network. For single parents the challenges that deployment presents is very different. If a single parent in the local military accommodation is deployed, myself and the various multi-disciplinary professionals that I work with, do our utmost to support the child, the parent and the temporary carer throughout the various stages of the cycle to reduce any familial trauma. If attachment theory, which includes the effects of a disrupted or broken attachment figure (Bowlby, 1969; Music, 2017), is taken into account it is likely that the effects of early childhood stress combined with the impact of broken attachment will have a deleterious effect on the development of many military children. The impact on the children of lone parents may then have a greater detrimental impact.

What we can learn NSPCC research supports these findings and provides examples of establishing specific voluntary school provision, such as a Military Munch lunchtime support group for pupils (McConnell et al., 2019). Reflective, research investigative skills may be used to gain detailed evidence on local, specific 'communities' as they adapt to change, such as refugee groups, travellers and corporate travellers. This can increase understanding of the needs of individual pupils and their families within a school setting. Also, building collaborative relationships with other health, social care and voluntary organization professionals has potential to produce more specific, relevant support (McConnell et al., 2019).

Know your families

'Attachment styles are ... not set in stone and can change with new experiences and new relationships, which should give hope to professionals and parents' (Music, 2017, p. 73). As pupils enter school and classrooms they bring with them relational experiences from home, both past and present, which can impact on immediate and long-term learning potential. Transition requires the development of new relational attachments, as between teacher and pupil (Ainsworth, 1991; Bowlby, 1969; Howe, 2011; Music, 2017). To support this, the extent to which a teacher can establish partnerships with parents may depend on the individual and their whole-school ethos, as well as parental commitment. Consider case study C below.

Case study C: 'Hard to Reach' families – perspectives from theory, professionals and a mother

Country: England

Age group: Adult

Setting: Children's Centre attached to a primary school

Participants involved: Children's centre manager (N), health visitor, mother

A conversation between a children's centre manager (N) and a health visitor assistant (former military wife and member of a wider multi-disciplinary team) raised the following question; why are the families of military personnel considered to be 'Hard to Reach'? A military family's deployment occurs in three stages: pre-deployment, deployment and post-deployment. Reflection of the manager's role and the support the centre offers leads to recognition that whilst the team are able to support these families with everyday life, they have a lack of first-hand experience into the events that occur when a family enters the differing stages of the 'deployment cycle'. A mother explains,

> We relocated due to my husband's job. We are a military family and were given just eight weeks' notice that we were going to be moved to London. We were a family of two girls and two dogs. Being placed in a top floor quarter with, at the time, two small children meant our dogs could not make the move with us. I struggled but eventually found a school for my eldest daughter. I looked into the local facilities and groups available for children. I attended a group for the military families in our local community centre. I went once! I'm not a confident person and not good at walking into a room and announcing my name, not one person spoke to me that day. So I thought I would try our local children's centre. Once again I went on my own, not knowing anyone and without any support from the military families. Again, no one spoke to me except the lady who ran the sessions, who made me feel very welcome. She spoke to my daughter and played with her and made me feel at ease. I continued to attend the group despite not enjoying it, but my daughter did. I felt judged as soon as I walked in through the door, for being the new person, for being an army person, or sadly the person with the child who was like a whirlwind. Without knowing my background or my child's background, people judged me. It wasn't until N was chatting to me one day, she knew where we lived and why my child was desperate to be outside. She got me! She didn't judge me. She was a comfort to me. It took a professional to see that I was lonely and I didn't have a naughty child. I had a child who came from a military background, who moved around a lot, had no local family network, whose daddy was not around half of the time and no garden to run around in and let off steam. Once N left, I stopped going to the

group and found other groups to attend, which is a shame because communities need children's centres to develop the community.

Knowing that N works in the school my girls attend, and that she 'gets them and me' is amazing.

Outcomes The mother values N, stating she 'got me!' N's professionalism, displayed within a 'chat', led to the mother feeling understood and confident in sending her children to the school where N went on to work. However, she, and her child, stayed away from the centre provision where she felt undervalued, judged and her child's behaviour misunderstood by other staff and parents.

What we can learn The creation of new relational attachments, through transition periods, is sensitive to informal and non-verbal, as well as formal, verbal communication (Music, 2017). Teachers have the potential to 'get' individuals/families, even from potential 'hard to reach' groups, so that they all feel valued and safe. Teachers need to know their families for who they are.

Reflective questions

1. What do you know about your pupils and their families?
2. How might you find out more about their communities?

Reflexive questions

1. Why do you know what you know about your pupils and their families?
2. What might be influencing your 'knowledge'?

Know your colleagues

'All involved in education will be motivated to find the ways that will work for this student learning this topic, and the results will be widely available in planning for future work' (Gardner, 1999, p. 154). Each staff member brings a unique perspective to teaching and relating to pupils, acknowledging autonomy but sometimes with a sense of isolation. Collaborative enquiry – planning and working with others – may prove beneficial for all as colleagues share knowledge and expertise constructively, but this requires specific communication skills that may not be owned by all (DeLuca, Bolden and Chan, 2017; Vangrieken et al., 2017). Consider how the challenges presenting in case study D below may be addressed.

Case study D: Dyslexia assessment

Country: England

Age group: Three adults

Setting: Primary school class – seven-year-olds

Participants involved: SPecific Literacy Difficulties (SPLD) teacher in training, class teacher (seven-year-olds), Special Educational Needs Coordinator

As a SPLD teacher in training, I recently received a referral from a Year 2 class teacher to carry out an initial specific assessment (Phab 2) (Gibbs and Bodman, 2014) with a 7-year-old girl, whom both teacher and parents felt was displaying dyslexic type tendencies. Prior to commencing the assessment, I perused her workbooks and observed her during a literacy lesson. Observations of workbook and class engagement showed a focused approach to learning, without additional support. I considered she was not dyslexic, but agreed, upon the teacher's request, to carry out the Phab 2 assessment (op. cit.). This took place in a designated room on a 1:1 basis. Here, her behaviour displayed anxiety not seen in the familiar classroom.

The results of this initial test confirmed that she did not display enough indicators of dyslexia to justify further testing. I discussed the findings of the six individual sections with the teacher, concluding the discussion by stating, 'I do not consider that the child is dyslexic'. The teacher responded, 'I don't believe these results. If ever a child was dyslexic, this child is.' This somewhat surprised me, showing that, in her opinion, this child definitely had dyslexia. I carried out the test, regardless of my initial professional judgement, as the teacher has many years teaching experience and was a highly regarded literacy leader. I was really offended by her reaction as, prior to this conversation, I had regarded her highly as a colleague. I discussed the power of her reaction and how I was left feeling with my line manager, highlighting that by reacting in this way she was doubting not only the validity of the test but also my professionalism. My line manager (the school's Special Educational Needs Co-ordinator) advised me to just forget about it and move on but several months later I was still shocked and upset by her remarks. Reflection into the discussion brought about the realisation that perhaps the words I used to describe the findings of the assessment caused the teacher to think that I was doubting her professional opinion in stating that a child that she felt was dyslexic was not, as a result she became defensive in her reaction.

Outcomes I will now report contradictory assessment findings to teachers by declaring that these results suggest a child does not have dyslexia, but this does not mean that he/she may not have a specific literacy difficulty. Then I will suggest we work together, as in sharing observations, in an attempt to identify where any difficulty may lie. If the child had demonstrated the same anxious behaviour in class as in 1:1 assessment, the teacher may have considered another referral route. There is definitely some barrier to this child achieving her full potential.

What we can learn Constructive, collaborative professional relationships require thoughtful and conscious use of vocabulary. Strong emotive responses require respectful acknowledgement (Beek, Zuiker and Zwart, 2018; DeLuca, Bolden and Chan, 2017; Vangrieken et al., 2017). A tentative suggestion, such as 'maybe', is more likely to promote constructive discussion than a definitive claim of 'this way'. In relation to context, teachers need to consider whether there are 'labels' which may influence decisions about what is 'best' for a pupil or pupils. They need to be aware of how different perceptions may have arisen and how differences may be respectfully considered to inform assessment processes. Teachers need to know how to effectively collaborate with their colleagues and build trusting relationships to enhance the learning and development of the pupils with whom they work.

Reflective questions

1. What did the SPLD teacher in training do to make sense of the reaction of the class teacher?
2. What was the result of this initial action?
3. How did she come to resolution?

Reflexive questions

1. How might this case study affect your responses and/or behaviours if faced with a similar situation?
2. What language might you use to ensure 'respectful acknowledgement' of another's professional judgement?

Know your professionals

Trust is enhanced by 'having the right people in the right place at the right time, and in the right frame of mind' (Gibbs, 2017, p. 7). No single discipline should be working in isolation when valuing the health, welfare and holistic development of children. Yet challenges may emerge when attempting to build interprofessional relationships. Government legislation and guidance is specific about 'everyone's responsibility' to work together in regard to safeguarding (DfE, 2019a) and this may be constructively extended to other pupil/family matters. The exemplar in case study E below demonstrates comparative perspectives.

Case study E: Establishing and/or spanning professional 'boundaries' – compare experiences voiced by a Child Centre Manager (F) and a class teacher (G)

Country: England

Age group: Adults

Setting: School-related

Participants involved: F – Child centre manager, G – class teacher

Narrative from F

I recognised that it was crucial to establish links with the Army Welfare Officer, responsible for working with these families. Cohesive working with the Army Welfare Service has resulted in a growing number of families accessing the services that are provided. Analysis of the support that the local children's centre offers these families, alongside my professional judgement, has brought about the realisation that family life for this particular group is very different to the non-military families living within the locality. Continuing discussions with a representative from the Army Welfare Service about what more I could do, highlighted that it is not unusual as a result of multiple deployments for the partner of a serving member of the military to take on the role of a single parent for up to 75% of the year.

Narrative from G

I share an occasion when I felt that my duty of care to a child, as class teacher, was compromised by a lack of access to direct communication from colleagues in other agencies: child A's parents were estranged and the mother had primary custody. During the summer before the child entered Year 6 the father kidnapped child A and removed him from the mother's care and presence. Thanks to The Hague Convention of 25 October 1980 on the Civil Aspects of International Child Abduction, an international hunt involving Interpol ensued and, some days later, child A was rescued. The child then spent a week in care abroad, while the courts unravelled who had responsibility for him, before he returned with his mother to the UK. After a week or so recovering from his ordeal at home, child A entered Year 6 (about a week after his peers). Throughout that academic year, the father remained a threat, even turning up at school and demanding a parent teacher consultation on one occasion. The police and social services were involved with the family. The head teacher (as the school's designated safeguarding lead) attended the multi-disciplinary meetings about child A, but I was not invited. Nor was any significant information from the meeting shared with me, either by the other agencies or the school's head teacher. Brayne, Carr and Goosey (2015, p. 186) agree that schools 'have a critical role in the protection of children'. I have more contact with the pupils I teach than any other professional, from any agency, and am bound by my Professional Standards, so obliged to treat any information confidentially.

Outcomes Teacher engagement through interprofessional relationships, as shown in F above, can enhance learning experiences for children. However, at times, as with G, frustration and potential conflict may arise, due to variations in personal, professional and/or interprofessional boundaries, perspectives, assumptions and expectations.

What we can learn 'Collaboration is not easy. It's not. In fact, it's really, really tricky. Just like any organisational change process, but probably more so, it requires significant planning, oversight and management, if it is to achieve the intended aims' (Gibbs, 2017, p. 3). A clear framework within each school context may be established for class teachers in regard to collaborative working with professionals outside, as well as within, the school community, referring to Keeping Children Safe in Education: for schools and colleges (DfE, 2019a). Teachers need to know other professionals and develop trusting relationships where information might be shared to provide appropriate support and intervention to enable pupils with different and diverse experience and needs, to thrive in learning and development.

Know your pupils

'From the perspective of care ethics, the teacher as carer is interested in the expressed needs of the cared-for, not simply the needs assumed by the school as an institution and the curriculum as a prescribed course of study' (Noddings, 2012, p. 772). While each teacher/pupil relationship is unique, the holistic nature of learning and development may not always be easy to monitor and sustain. Relational pedagogy may increase empathic communication and strengthen attachment (Goleman, 2006; Music, 2017; Reeves and Le Mare, 2017). However numerous variables are present and influential. The length of time a pupil spends in the classroom and school may provide valuable nurturing opportunities or identify specific needs for early intervention within a whole school approach (DfE, 2018b).

Within a large secondary school, a non-teaching head of year shares a specific brief to acknowledge this, demonstrating a need for collaborative working with colleagues, pupils and their parents/carers.

Case study F: Relationships

Country: England

Age group: Secondary

Setting: Large city secondary academy school

Participants involved: Head of Year 8, non-teaching, ex-pupil

This role is heavily focused on building relationships with young people themselves, and also their parents. I take responsibility for any issue that arises relating to the 206 Year 8 students in the school, be that their emotional wellbeing, behaviour, safeguarding, attendance, achievement or anything else that falls in between. Apart from two hours a day, which are spent supervising the independent learning room or being on call for whole school behaviour issues in classrooms, my working day is largely flexible. Although the majority of that time is spent reacting to issues that arise, there is also time for proactive work – dropping into lessons to check on various students, meeting students 1-2-1 and even small-scale interventions such as reading groups. An added benefit is that I will remain with my year group for 5 years as they pass from Year 7 to 11. Inevitably I will see the students through some of their best and worst times, able to build a long-term, trusting relationship with the ability for me to speak into their situations and guide them through school.

A challenge in building and sustaining relationships in my role is the pure number of students in my year group. Previously there were also assistant heads of year, meaning more 'hands-on deck' to deal with any issues that arose and also to work more proactively. However, funding cuts and increases in year group size due to a population bulge in the city means that I am pulled in many directions. Ultimately, a large proportion of my time is taken up with the ten or so students whose behaviour is most difficult to manage. Although I build strong relationships with these children, I am aware that there are a vast number who do not get as much time and attention.

It can also be difficult to get other staff to 'buy in' to building relationships with students who can be incredibly challenging in the classroom, such as J in my year group. J is currently being assessed for Autistic Spectrum Disorder and having worked closely with him and his mother for a year, I now know the best and worst ways to deal with him. Although I have circulated this information to staff, it has still been challenging as his teachers, who see a huge number of students, struggle to implement strategies and differentiate for J alongside the 30 others in the classroom. A number of these students will also have their own Special Educational Needs or Social, Emotional and Mental Health needs. To complicate matters, J can be more challenging for teachers who he perceives do not understand him and therefore does not like. This leads to more issues in these lessons and unless that member of staff has bought into the strategies enough to know how to react in that situation, there is a vicious circle of J's perceptions being reinforced and therefore more difficult to challenge.

Outcomes My relationships with students mean that they feel able to come and speak to me about problems in the classroom and often I find that I act as a mediator between a student and a member of staff. Due to my relationships with students, I am able to challenge them about their behaviour in classrooms and generally they will listen. They trust me and therefore listen, even if they may not like what they are being told.

My role uniquely places me as the link between the student, their parents and the wider staff body. It has been as important to build relationships and trust with parents as it has been with their children. Parents feel able to ring me and discuss concerns that they have about their child, or concerns about the school. With the most challenging students, it is of pivotal importance to involve their parents in the process. Young people respond best to consistency and without parental support, in my experience, it is very difficult to get anything to change.

Listening is a key tool in developing relationships with students. It can be very easy to dismiss or belittle problems raised by a 12-year-old student. However, doing so instead of just listening can be very harmful to building a relationship. I always try and remind myself (however difficult it sometimes is!) what it was like to be that age and that the student in front of me does not have the same frames of reference as I do with the benefit of age and experience. Although it is easy enough for me to dismiss a Year 8 girl's sadness about her 'best friend' not inviting her to a sleepover, for her it may possibly be the worst thing that has ever happened. Wading in with 'everything will be fine' or 'just ignore it' can do more harm than good. Sitting and listening, then trying to encourage her, builds that trust.

A huge benefit of the non-teaching head of year role is that of time. Although I definitely don't have as much time as I would like, the fact that I don't have to teach means that I am more available to students, so able to build meaningful relationships.

Secondary – ex-pupil's voice

My time at secondary school was made immeasurably more bearable thanks to high quality pastoral care. The ability to speak freely about problems and ideas to someone I trusted was invaluable. I often struggled socially at school and my mental health was suffering as a result. The support I received during this important stage of my life and my education enabled me to develop a level of resilience and a more positive self-esteem. Despite attending a Christian school the support I received was based on a variety of cultures and traditions.

What we can learn The teacher's role in this case study was to be a trusted pastoral support to pupils. Despite the challenges of working with large numbers of pupils in the school, the teacher formed professional relationships that enabled the children and young people to share their concerns. The teacher listened to the pupils and took their concerns seriously. 'Receptive listening is the very heart of caring relations. It is also … a powerful strategy for learning' (Noddings, 2012, p. 780). Time for receptive listening enables expressed, rather than just assumed, needs to be heard (ibid.). While curriculum content increasingly seeks to enhance knowledge and understanding of relational, social and emotional development, mental well-being concerns remain high (Children's Society, 2019; DfE, 2019b). The value of having a trusted professional who listens is highlighted in the comments of the ex-pupil. Teachers need to recognize the significance of knowing their pupils, to listen to them so that optimal conditions for their unique learning and development might be achieved (see Chapter 6).

The relevance of having a whole school collaborative ethos has been discussed, and is extended in the 'Window on research' section below (Reeves and Le Mare, 2017). The Canadian research study explores how teachers may use a professional, collaborative 'relationship lens' in the classroom. Initial teacher training and CPD may also provide opportunities to develop such collaborative communication skills.

Reflective questions

1. When did you last 'listen' to a pupil or group of pupils?
2. What did you learn? How did you respond?

Reflexive questions

1. What might affect what you hear: essentially, what you might choose to hear?
2. How might you be more actively alert to what pupils actually say?

Window on research

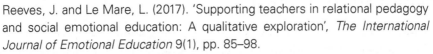

Reeves, J. and Le Mare, L. (2017). 'Supporting teachers in relational pedagogy and social emotional education: A qualitative exploration', *The International Journal of Emotional Education* 9(1), pp. 85–98.

Relational pedagogy is defined in this small-scale study as 'teachers who are aware of, and explicitly focus on, the quality of their interactions with students to develop classroom communities that promote academic, social and emotional growth' (Reeves and Le Mare, 2017, p. 6). Three teachers attempt to use relational pedagogy within daily classroom/school practice, while engaging with external group support, including input on attachment (Ainsworth et al., 1978) and care (Noddings, 2012) theories. Reflective journal entries maintained throughout the research presented seven themes:

- Commitment to relational pedagogy, even when it may be 'difficult to go against the flow in the workplace and stand up to colleagues' (p. 94)
- Hesitancy regarding commitment of time for dialogue
- Missed opportunities – leading to the involvement of other professional resources
- Abandoning relational pedagogy – using organization disciplinary strategies with challenging behaviour
- Reflection on mistakes – increased realization of valuing collaboration with children
- Isolation – 'teachers began to see the impact that collaborating with like-minded staff in their own schools would have on creating caring relationships' (p. 94)
- Success

Implications of this research:

Relational pedagogy is likely to be best supported by a whole-school approach with:

- time and opportunity for staff training/discussion on creating knowledgeable, caring, responsible citizens within the aims of education
- formalized conversations regarding teachers' feelings and beliefs about their relationships with pupils, encouraging teachers to look at ways to enhance pupil/teacher relationships
- support and encouragement for teachers to visit each other's classes
- co-planning/co-teaching – bringing teachers together rather than isolated, with a need to timetable within organizational structure.

Know your collaborative professional relationships in practice

'The way ahead is for a presumption of trust to be the guiding principle at every level of the education system' (Seldon, 2009, p. 155). A range of professional relationships has been shared in this chapter so far, highlighting strengths and challenges. Where trust has been evident and collaboration has been constructive, the outcomes for the children, families and professionals concerned have been enhanced. The final case study G provides additional strategies that may encourage you to engage in developing collaborative professional relationships within your school or setting.

Case study G: Collaborative learning experiences

Country: England

Age group: Adults

Setting: Two primary schools (five to eleven years)

Participants involved: Newly qualified teacher (NQT), middle manager

NQT narrative

The huge advantage of training though the Schools Direct programme (DfE, 2018a) is that you are working alongside experienced teachers every day who have specialised knowledge in the many facets of education. There is no scenario or challenge that hasn't previously been addressed and overcome, and this pool of experience and knowledge is a vital resource that you can, and should, tap into.

Throughout my training, I experienced a level of collaboration that would be envied by many industries. Whilst curriculums change, the progress and attainment of pupils remains at the heart of each professional's practice and that includes working closely with colleagues to make sure all children achieve their potential.

Middle management leader

The school's ethos focuses on the importance of building a strong team around the child to ensure that they have the vital tools, skills and knowledge to prepare them to be an influential member of society with a rich foundation to achieve their full potential. With a clear ethos, it is easy for all members of staff to create the best learning environment possible for pupils. In order to carry out this ethos successfully, the school must ensure that it has a committed team who are willing to work together and believe in the same goal; furthermore, this circle of interest needs to be shared and believed by outer circles: parents and carers. As a middle manager it is my role to lead my team well in order to provide pupils with an educational journey that will prepare them for their future. As part of a consistent approach throughout the school, we have regular team meetings, training days, coaching sessions and parental engagement days to encourage as much interaction and involvement as possible. Living and working in an era where technology provides us with ease, convenience and the ability to multi-task, my team and I proudly embrace tools such as 'Behaviour Watch' as a learning platform. Such interactive tools enable schools to strengthen collaboration with the team around the child.

Outcomes With the use of social media such as Twitter, blogging, school websites and apps such as SeeSaw, teaching staff are now able to share pupils' learning with parents and carers instantly. It would be naïve to believe that technology is unnecessary when we are preparing children for the future. With this in mind, like any new or unfamiliar tool, there are dangers of the misuse of using the internet as a tool. However, instead of creating barriers, a school may educate staff, pupils, parents and carers to use technology safely, including how to deal with potential dangers.

What we can learn 'We have to ask questions and reflect on the answers. Dialogue is fundamental in building relations of care and trust' (Noddings, 2012, p. 775). All of the above would not be possible without a team willing to work together and dedicate their time to identify areas of need and create effective and appropriate provisions for children and young people. 'Collaborative capacity' (Gibbs, 2017, p. 5) depends on teachers' willingness and ability to shed some autonomy, or lose some relative strength. Each school and setting community may seek to develop a range of collaborative opportunities that can build and sustain trust (DeLuca, Bolden and Chan, 2017, Vangrieken et al., 2017).

Implications for teachers

Although the focus of this chapter has concerned the cultivation of adult professional, collaborative relationships, all examples cited have illustrated how these may significantly impact upon the development and learning experiences of children and young people. There is a sense of dedication for enhanced, constructive, lifelong learning for each pupil. The energy and commitment of those who have shared their narratives have been evident through the case studies – with a willingness of professionals to model continuous development, creativity and trust, whilst honestly addressing differences and engaging with challenges. Formal and informal opportunities to collaborate are evident which may encourage a sense of belonging for teachers, families and pupils – an environment for relational pedagogy to thrive. The case studies in this chapter also recognize personal and professional challenges that may be encountered when willing to collaborate with colleagues and other professionals to enhance learning opportunities for pupils. When engaging with potential ethical and moral dilemmas, teachers have acknowledged their vulnerability and possible sense of isolation, while valuing peer and specialist support when available. They truly show that, when given the opportunities, they continue to build a real vision of 'professional capital' comprising 'human capital (the talent of individuals); social capital (the collaborative power of the group); and decisional capital (the wisdom and expertise to make sound judgements about learners that are cultivated over many years)' (Hargreaves and Fullan, 2013, p. 37).

Reflective questions

As a professional how do you engage with the core themes of this chapter:

1. that, to enhance learning, it is a professional responsibility to ensure that you come to know your pupils and their unique contexts beyond the school setting.
2. that working collaboratively informs quality planning and assessment, resulting in pupil achievement and progression.

Reflexive question

As a professional how do you engage with these core themes in relation to your own emotions and assumptions and biases?

Annotated bibliography

Music, G. (2017). *Nurturing natures – Attachment and children's emotional, sociocultural and brain development.* **2nd edn. London: Routledge**.
A detailed, challenging, accessible reference resource that combines theories and research from neuroscience, developmental psychology and cross-cultural studies to inform, support and encourage teaching and learning across the age range.

Relationship Foundation (2019). '*Teachers get by with a little help from their friends.* Available at: https://relationshipsfoundation.org/events/in-the-news/teachers-get-by-with-a-little-help-from-their-friends/.

Current research identifies the impact of strong social and professional relationships on trainee teachers' retention and performance.

Vangrieken, K., Grosemans, I., Dochy, F. and Kyndt, E. (2017). 'Teacher autonomy and collaboration: A paradox? Conceptualising and measuring teacher's autonomy and collaborative attitude', *Teaching and Teacher Education*, **67, pp. 302–15.**
Belgian research that challenges teacher identity and highlights potential for collaborative professional relationships.

8

Resilience, Reflection and Reflexivity

Daryl Maisey and Catherine Warnock

Introduction

For any teacher who has undergone training to gain a professional status, the phrase to be 'critically reflective in practice' is probably very familiar. Teachers are encouraged to be reflective and reflexive professionals: the notion that these are essential elements in order to enable effective practice. In addition, teachers are tasked with being resilient – that in the face of challenge or difficulty there is the ability and capability to be robust and buoyant. Teachers will bounce back regardless. However, when exploring these terms with trainee and experienced teachers it becomes apparent that whilst some commonalities of understanding may exist, the terms have quite different and varied interpretations. Theories and related literature concerning these notions affirm the multiplicity of understandings that have developed over time (Brookfield, 1995; Dewey, 1933; Fook and Gardner, 2007; Mezirow, 1990; Schön, 1983). Therefore, it could be argued that these notions might each be described as illusive descriptors of complex phenomena. So it is at this point that we start the chapter!

As authors, it is our intention to explore and reveal some of the meanings associated with the terms *reflection*, *reflexivity* and *resilience* and how they might support, challenge and impact upon the personal, social and emotional states of teachers. The chapter draws attention to the role of reflection and reflexivity in resilience – how these might facilitate teachers to manage thoughts, ideas and emotions in order to shape reactions and guide responses to everyday encounters and situations in professional practice. Case studies are used to illustrate how reflection and reflexivity and a teacher's resilience impact upon the learning experiences and development of children. The chapter starts with a brief exploration of these key terms and how they are situated within the discourse of a teacher's professional practice.

Meanings and definitions

Dewey (1933) is considered to be one of the first influential contributors to the conceptual understanding of reflection in professional practice. In his original work he outlines concern for what he calls *routine* rather than *intelligent* or *reflective* thoughts and actions. Dewey (1933, p. 9) explains that routine thoughts and actions are influenced and guided by habits and traditions, whereas reflective thoughts and actions are seen as 'active, persistent, and careful consideration of any belief or supposed form of knowledge in the light of the grounds that support it'. Routine action might be presented as the teacher who accepts that their responses to issues in practice may have already been defined for them by known assumptions, authority or institutional expectations (i.e. routine or habitual responses). Reflective action requires teachers to engage in critical, evidence informed analysis of their experiences. This requires them to have a conscious alertness to what they are thinking and doing. The following case study provides an example of where a secondary school science teacher describes a shift in the way he thinks about his teaching from a routine to a more reflective position.

Case study: Thinking differently

Country: England

Age group: Eleven to sixteen years

Setting: Secondary school

Participants involved: Secondary science teacher and higher education teacher educator

Jay is a science teacher in a large urban secondary school in the south-east of England. He has been working as a science teacher for five years with children aged from eleven to sixteen years. Jay has begun to mentor trainee teachers from the local Higher Education Initial Teacher Training provider. As part of his new mentor role, Jay has attended training that has included the exploration of research and theory concerning different and diverse pedagogical approaches to science education. In addition, training has included how to support trainee teachers in developing reflective and reflexive practice. Following one of the sessions, Jay engages the tutor in dialogue about his own practice. He reveals that from his new learning he recognizes how his practice has been heavily influenced by institutional expectations: that he has adopted the practices of others in his school without question. He discusses how little his teaching has developed over time and expresses remorse that he has been unresponsive to new ways of working that might have benefitted the pupils in his classes. In his words,

I feel guilty. I've only taught from what I have known and seen others do. I remember being told 'this is how we do it' and so I followed that. I used what I was given and copied how others worked. Now I can see I could have done things a bit differently, kept up with new ideas and resources in science education. I could have asked to go to other schools and see how they did things, how others taught it, but never gave it time. I am not sure whether I have always been as good a teacher as I thought.

Outcomes Jay has recognized that his new learning about science education and reflective practice has affected his perceptions and ways of thinking about effective teaching. He has indicated that his new knowledge about pedagogy in science education has provided the means by which 'careful consideration' (Dewey, 1933) might be applied. Jay has demonstrated alertness to some of the influences that might have shaped his practice.

What we can learn By Dewey's (1933) definition, Jay appears to have been embroiled in routine action. By his own admission he has adopted, without question, the habits, routines and expectations of the institution in which he works, influenced by those working with him. In his dialogue Jay reveals a shift towards reflective action: a self-appraisal and a willingness to develop, supported by new knowledge and research evidence of effective pedagogy in science education. Jay's example indicates that teachers at different points of their career might come to appreciate their ways of thinking, and by doing that, they may positively and directly affect the pupils with whom they work.

Whilst Dewey (1933) proposes that some routine actions may be appropriate, he suggests reflection as the means to break free of assumptions and habits that may not always be conducive to effective practice.

> Reflection emancipates us from merely impulsive and merely routine activity, it enables us to direct our activities with foresight and to plan according to ends-in-view or purposes of which we are aware, to act in deliberate and intentional fashion, to know what we are about when we act.
>
> (Dewey, 1933, p. 17)

In practice, teachers may perceive that they are engaging in reflective practice as they try to solve problems or issues in everyday situations. However, actions may be largely known, mundane, expected or directed. They may not be unique to the context, individuals or groups involved. They may not consider the exploration of other possibilities. They may not include the examination of factors influencing reactions, responses, decisions and actions. Dewey advocates the need for systematic reflections of teaching: for teachers, this is to show awareness of unique experiences and to develop practice as a result.

Schön (1983) develops the ideas of Dewey to provide some insight into the use of knowledge and/or experience when professionals are engaged in *reflection-in-action* and *reflection-on-action*. Schön (1983) distinguishes between reflections that involve immediate intuitive responses and those that involve thinking retrospectively. His work examines the notion of intuitive practice as a form of knowledge: how teachers think in the moment, are alert to knowledge inhabiting their thoughts, influencing their behaviours and how their reflections-in-action might affect outcomes. Identifying the complexity and uniqueness of professional practice, Schön (1983) articulates that the process of systematic reflection-in-action and reflection-on-action requires 'professional artistry'. He explains this as a kind of competence, where professionals engage in problematizing rather than solving issues, leading to affirmation of existing practices as well as revealing new possibilities in meaning, understanding and behaviours. As Thompson and Pascal (2012, p. 314) explain, 'Professional practice is not a technical process of applying (scientifically derived) solutions to practice problems. More realistically, it is a matter of wrestling with the complexities of both theory and practice, using professional artistry to move forward as effectively as possible.' Professionals demonstrate actions by way of looking forwards and backwards at their experiences, examining what is known about the issue/problem/situation and what is not known. It is this exploration that leads to development.

This notion of problematizing issues may not always sit comfortably with teachers. There may well be tensions if teachers perceive their role as one of finding solutions and/or generating certainties in practice – the drive to know what will work to produce defined outcomes. Accepting that teaching and learning are unpredictable, due to the diversity of context and the individuals with whom teachers work, is challenging. Teachers want to know if there are tried and tested ways of working that will ensure all pupils will learn and make progress, satisfying potential ideologies. However, acknowledging that professional practice is uncertain might provide the means by which teachers think differently.

If there is recognition that there are multiple ways of achieving a solution or outcomes, then teaching and learning become emancipatory (Dewey, 1933) and reflection becomes the means of learning. As Johns (1995) suggests, the process of reflection may result in an individual experiencing a change of state, in perspective and/or learning. The teacher is alert to the need to explore alternative possibilities and not to accept the routine or mundane. The teacher is attentive to examine new theoretical understandings of their area of focus, to explore different pedagogical approaches and to acknowledge that as a result, their own presuppositions and assumptions may be challenged. This approach requires teachers to confront potential susceptibilities. If teachers believe that their ways of doing and being are always effective, then challenging 'the self' in this context may result in tensions with ideologies that may be both personal and professional. In one sense this requires teachers to be aware of, and acknowledge, their own vulnerabilities in professional practice – that what teachers might consider to be effective in one context, for a particular purpose, in a specific timeframe, may indeed be shown to be ineffective as new knowledge is subsequently developed. It is to accept that whilst teachers may constantly strive to be effective in practice, they operate within a changing political, social and temporal context. Teachers may find that their endeavours might not always have the desired outcomes. There isn't one way of achieving looked-for results and things tried in practice might not always work! External and internal factors are present and influential in affecting how teachers practise and how pupils learn. Teachers should not 'feel guilty' as Jay expressed in the case study above, but they should recognize the complexity of professional practice and their role within it.

Reflective questions

1. Can you think of a situation where you have consciously changed the way you have typically carried out your practice?
2. What was the catalyst for this change?

Reflexive questions

1. Did you have to challenge your own knowledge or ways of doing things to make the change?
2. How did the change make you feel/why?

Assumptions

Mezirow (1998) suggests that reflection is more than just thinking about what happens in practice. It is about critiquing assumptions and that 'is central to understanding how adults learn to think for themselves rather than act on the concepts, values, and feelings of others' (Mezirow, 1998, p. 185). Thinking about Jay in the case study above, Mezirow's position suggests that Jay might have come into some conflict between his acceptance to teach in the image of others and the ways in which he might have chosen to teach had he been in different circumstances. However, teachers need to be aware that their pedagogical choices and behaviours in practice are very likely to mirror those of others in their school environment.

Siebert and Costley (2013) caution that the values and beliefs a professional holds will be influenced and affected by the organization in which they work. The suggestion is that teachers should not be surprised that they adopt practices, habits, routines and behaviours expected of them in the context of their unique schools. However, they may be concerned when those practices become mundane or when they might generate tensions with personal aspirations and ideologies. Schön (1983, p. 337) cautions that conflict inevitably exists as teachers examine their position in the discourse of 'bureaucracy and professionalism'. Personal and professional values and beliefs may differ between teachers in the same school and between teachers and their schools. However, they will inhabit behaviours. Teachers need to be attentive to how their values and beliefs have been formed, shaped and influenced through their diverse and unique life experiences (Mezirow, 1998). Teaching is not without challenge but that challenge may be in the exploration of selfhood. Brookfield (1995, p. 1) suggests,

> One of the hardest things teachers learn is that the sincerity of their intentions does not guarantee the purity of their practice. The cultural, psychological and political complexities of learning, and the ways in which power complicates all human relationships (including those between students and teachers) means that teaching can never be innocent.

Brookfield (1995) explains that teaching innocently is when teachers do not call into question the reasons why they do what they do and why pupils might or might not always respond as expected. He argues that reflection can be understood as 'assumption hunting' and this relates to the notion of reflexivity.

Reflexivity

> Reflection becomes reflexivity when informed and intentional internal dialogue leads to changes in educational practices, expectations, and beliefs. Reflexivity can promote deep professional learning and bring sustainable change in education.
>
> (Feucht, Brownlee and Schraw, 2017, p. 234)

In this definition, reflexivity is perceived as a conscious change in behaviours that can lead to transformative practice. Therefore, as a personal endeavour, reflexivity is affected by the values and beliefs held by individuals. The suggestion is that the ways by which teachers interpret information and make sense of situations are shaped by their personal biographies. Their historical narratives as derived from social, cultural and political influence over time affect the approaches and meanings that they attach to professional practices. Brookfield (1995) explains that these narratives can become 'taken for granted' and give 'meaning and purpose' to a teacher's identity and 'common sense' practice. They are not routinely questioned for fear of complicating the status quo. Consider why you, as the teacher, would want to question something that you have always believed in or undertaken with purposeful intent that might require a change of approach. Why would you want to expose a strongly held belief that might mean changing your behaviours and ways of doing things in front of others? It may be easier to accept what is known and comfortable and mundane. As a simple analogy, consider that adults like to cross their arms the same way and without question, as it does not require attentive thinking. However, Brookfield (1995) strongly advocates the need for teachers to question their assumptions. As a professional responsibility, seeking and critically challenging 'common sense' assumptions can lead to an understanding that when a teacher's experience is not positive (such as a lesson that has not gone to plan), there are multiple possibilities and/or explanations. It is not that the teacher has failed. As Brookfield explains,

> Since we rarely have full awareness of what we're doing, and since we frequently misread how others perceive our actions, an uncritical stance towards our practice sets us up for a lifetime of frustration.
>
> (Brookfield, 1995, p. 1)

Being conscious of factors influencing teachers' behaviours and actions relates to the attributes of reflection described by Dewey (1933) as the need to be open-minded, responsible, wholehearted and direct. Open-minded as a way of listening to and appreciating different and alternative views; responsible in ensuring careful consideration of the implications and impact of any actions; wholehearted as the means by which teachers might overcome uncertainties and are committed to making meaningful change to practice – a sense of resilience; and direct in that reflection and its consequences are worth practising to enable transformation (Pollard, 2019, p. 90).

Teachers are exposed to different situations, encounters and experiences every day. The very nature of teaching and learning as a social venture, suggests unpredictability. For teachers this can be both liberating and unnerving. Dewey (1933) and Schön (1983) advocate the need for teachers to think beyond the obvious and to adopt a more curious and investigative approach to their practice. The suggestion is that teachers should not dwell on problems that may not be resolved or reconcilable, and that indicate some element of failure and blame, but should embrace transformative learning with alertness to factors that inhabit and influence contexts. As Fook and Askeland (2006, p. 45) explain,

> Reflexivity can simply be defined as an ability to recognize our own influence – and the influence of our social and cultural contexts on research, the type of knowledge we

create, and the way we create it (Fook 1999b). In this sense, then, it is about factoring ourselves as players into the situations we practice in.

This analogy is helpful in understanding the wider contextual influences that are present as teachers make sense of practice. Teachers new to the profession should be aware of their 'espoused theories' and 'theories in use'. Espoused theories are what teachers believe should be happening in practice, as formally learnt in training courses, what they aspire to do and what they use to explain actions. Theories-in-use are what actually happens in practice in response to expectations and demands placed on them that might be in conflict with their espoused theories (Argyris and Schön, 1974). If unchallenged, Eraut (2002) cautions that theories-in-use can remain unexamined and some routine behaviours may then become 'dysfunctional'.

Reflection and reflexivity enable implicit theories-in-action to be made explicit and 'pulls the practitioner out of the "automatic pilot" mode of skillful behavior' (Eraut, 1994, p. 144). This alertness to the everydayness of a teacher's actions and behaviours can be the catalyst for ongoing personal and professional learning. 'If professional development is to bring about lasting change it must involve the teachers concerned in analysing, critiquing, reflecting upon, and improving their own classroom practice' (Harnett, 2012, p. 382). However, Eraut (2000) suggests that this should not be an isolated activity. Whilst there is the suggestion that teachers should have a personal responsibility to question their own practice and have awareness of factors influencing their behaviours, there is the notion that this may also involve social complexities. Reflection and reflexivity might involve both individual and social venture.

Window on research

Kramer, M. (2018). 'Promoting teachers' agency: Reflective practice as transformative disposition', *Reflective Practice: International and Multidisciplinary Perspectives*, 19(2), pp. 211–24.

Kramer uses formative interventionalist methodology to explore how reflective practice might be conceptualized as extending beyond the individual teacher. He suggests that the theory of expansive learning based on existentialist core assumptions and compatibility with cultural-historical activity theory can provide a framework for 'collaborative reflective practice with a transformative disposition' (Kramer, 2018, p. 212) in order to encourage both individual and collective professional development. Contextualized in a small secondary school in Austria, Kramer (2018, p. 223) argues that 'reflective practice and transformative agency go hand in hand in a joint activity'.

Collaborative learning

Pollard (2019, p. 93) suggests, 'Reflective teaching, professional learning and personal fulfillment are enhanced through collaboration and dialogue with colleagues.' Teachers new to the profession, or more experienced teachers undertaking training courses, may well recognize pedagogical approaches in their professional learning, where dialogue with experienced and knowledgeable 'others' is facilitated. The argument is that reflection should be a collective endeavour.

> The social context is a primary feature of human reality. There is therefore a need to see personal reflection as not only an interpersonal matter, but also as part of the broader context of cultural formations and structural relations.
>
> (Thompson and Pascal, 2011, pp. 16–17)

Eraut (2000) explains that dialogue between work colleagues can be a supportive way to reveal theories-in-use and to challenge discrepancies with espoused theories. By working together teachers can reveal routine behaviours and the potential for dysfunctional practice. Teachers have the opportunity to share knowledge and expertise in the reflective process of making the implicit explicit, leading to what Dewey calls a 'reconstruction of experience' (1933, p. 87) as they transform their approaches to teaching. However, reflecting with others is not without challenge. Research undertaken in school contexts (Leithwood, Steinbach and Ryan, 1997, Nias, 1998) indicates that teachers struggle to find a balance between reflecting on practice that challenges assumptions and presuppositions, and the need to maintain positive relationships and avoid conflict. Teachers do not want to upset their colleagues by suggesting that the ways in which they practise might not be effective. However, McCotter (2001) argues that generating the conditions by which teachers can engage in collective reflection is possible and refers to the need for safe spaces, where teachers can reflect together without judgement.

> The collegial support that results from communal reflection helps empower each one of us to make sound professional decisions designed to counter hegemonic elements present in schools. Persistent critique is also part of the group's reflection and dialogue. That critique helps us to gain more and different perspectives on the contexts in which we work, and the part we play in that environment.
>
> (McCotter, 2001, p. 702)

McCotter (2001) suggests that a collaborative approach to reflection enables teachers to be challenged to look at, and beyond themselves, developing awareness of the social and political dimensions affecting their practice. Kemmis (2006, p. 474) also argues (in the context of action research) that collaborative reflections can facilitate the examination of 'unwelcome truths'. He suggests that transforming practice is not only an individual endeavour but requires teachers to challenge and change the understandings of others 'who share in the constitution of social and educational practices by their thought and action' (ibid.). The indication is that collective reflection in a safe and respectful environment may enable teachers to address assumptions, problematize concerns and transform their practice together.

> ## Reflective questions
>
> 1. Can you recall an issue or problem in your school that was resolved by collaborative reflection with other professional colleagues?
> 2. How was the issue resolved?

> ## Reflexive questions
>
> 1. What were your assumptions and presuppositions that were challenged in the process of resolving the issue/problem?
> 2. What were your actions/behaviours that required change?

Collective reflection to resolve challenges requires teachers to invest effort, with the potential for exposure to public criticism or endorsement of effective practice. Inevitably, this carries an emotional dimension. In the last section of this chapter the significance of emotional demands in professional practice is explored. Examples of teachers' experiences are drawn on to illustrate how behaviours may be affected and how reflection and reflexivity 'involves a degree of "unlearning" and abandoning previously held beliefs and values' (Thompson and Pascal, 2012, p. 318) which in itself is emotionally demanding, requiring the resilience of teams and individuals.

Reflection and emotions

Emotional resilience is key in a teacher's role. It is 'our individual capacity to cope with adversity in life' (Barry, 2018, p. 11). Explanations of emotions and how they manifest in professional practice are multi-faceted but Barry (2018, p. 12) provides a simple description that suggests emotions relate to 'how we feel, lasting for relatively short durations, usually minutes to hours. If they last for a longer period, we call them moods. Some experts join emotions and moods together calling them feelings'. Teachers in their day-to-day practice might experience both positive and negative emotions. There may be times of joy, happiness, pleasure, contentment and peacefulness, and also anger, frustration, fear, guilt, hurt and sadness. These emotions may affect a teacher's perspective of practice, producing an affirming sense of fulfilment and reward but also anxiety and concern about their capabilities. As Hargreaves (2000, p. 812) explains, 'Emotions are not peripheral to people's lives; nor can they be compartmentalized away from action or from rational reflection within these lives. Emotion, cognition and action, in fact, are integrally connected.' Emotions are a part of who teachers are, and they are represented in their professional conduct.

Teachers are constantly 'thinking and making decisions – thinking is shown in constant interaction with doing and communicating' (Eraut, 2004, p. 257). Barry (2018, p. 11) explains, 'Emotions are important as they are the junction points between our thoughts and behaviour.' It is what teachers are feeling that may be demonstrated in the classroom through their actions and behaviours. However, teachers are tasked with putting on a positive daily performance, a mask, a public display, as expected of a professional with responsibility for pupils. Some emotions and feelings may not be overtly or explicitly displayed regardless of how the teacher might actually feel. Hochschild (1983, p. 7) suggests this might be described as 'emotional labor' – this being the 'the management of feeling to create a publicly observable facial and bodily display'. In effect, it might be described as a teaching act that is put on within the classroom to fulfil the teacher persona – the daily performance. Here the expectation is for the teacher to be a calm, confident, communicative and professional individual, who is the constant in an ever-changing, uncertain world. However, there are many factors that influence what happens in the classroom that might affect a teacher's emotional responses. These include the school environment (space and facilities), the teacher's health and well-being (see Chapter 3), the weather, support staff, the school leadership team, budget, curriculum expectations, school inspection, outside agencies and parental involvement. The following case study reveals some of the influencing factors present as a teacher examines her responses to emotional demands experienced when working with parents/carers of pupils in her class.

Case study: Emotional responses to working with parents/carers

Country: England

Age group: Five to eleven years

Setting: Primary school

Participant involved: Primary school teacher

Parents, in my experience, present different emotional demands on me. There are the new parents, who need nurture and guidance in supporting their child's learning and who often work with me for the benefit of their children. I spend time listening to their concerns and worries and building up their trust and confidence. Sometimes I am tired at the end of the day but I know it's important for them to have my reassurance that their child is ok. There are experienced parents who have done it before and 'know the ropes'. They can generally be fully supportive and engaged or quite nonchalant, but in a trusting kind of way. These parents present different demands on me that can sometimes cause frustrations. These parents often have multiple communications to and from teachers, particularly if they have children in different year groups and at different schools. In my experience I am usually able to manage any issues and build a reciprocal relationship with these parents. But I have to work hard to help them understand that not all teachers and schools have the same systems and expectations. Messages between schools and parents can get lost or misunderstood. These parents can sometimes take their frustrations out on me, acting crossly and talking abruptly. I know this is not directed at me personally and I know that it's because they are annoyed, but I can't say 'this isn't my fault!' I have to be calm, apologise and diffuse their frustrations. This can be pretty exhausting but it keeps the relationship going. For me, the most challenging situations emotionally are where the expectations of parents are different to the ways of working in the school. This can result in unreasonable demands on the school and especially on me. At times I have struggled to make positive and reciprocal relationships. I find it emotionally really difficult. I want to get them on side. I want to work with them so that we can fully support their child's learning but different understandings of how children learn, and why we do what we do, can make this really hard work. I can experience feelings of frustration and I have to work hard not to show them. I think I also get upset that these parents don't seem to trust me.

Outcomes Teaching is a social endeavour so it is not unexpected that there may well be tensions as teachers experience situations and encounters with others in varied social contexts. Inevitably, emotions inhabit practice. However, behaviours and conduct in these contexts require teachers to act with professional integrity and with control. This can be emotionally demanding. Teaching is emotional.

What can we learn The classroom reality can be very challenging. Hargreaves (2000, p. 814) suggests that teachers 'manufacture and mask their emotions, when they enthuse about a new initiative, are overjoyed at a student breakthrough, show patience with a frustrating colleague, or are calm in the face of parental criticism'. They probably feel very differently. In classroom teaching, a teacher's emotions are not always natural but are controlled: an act, which in itself requires and engages the emotions. Teachers learn to manage their own emotions as they manage the emotions of others (Hochschild, 1983).

Research by Hargreaves (2000, p. 814) examines 'how the emotional character of teaching is influenced and shaped by teachers' lives and identities on the one hand, and the changing conditions of their work on the other'. His findings suggest that emotions can be both 'harmful' and 'helpful', and are intrinsically linked to relationships teachers have with others. Hargreaves (2000, p. 184) suggests that for teachers to 'use their emotions well in the workplace depends on two other things in addition to individual emotional competence: what people's jobs or professions expect of them emotionally, and how their organisation structures human interactions in ways that help or hinder emotional expression and understanding'. A teacher's social world is the context in which these integrally connected notions are present. Bronfenbrenner's Socio-ecological model (1979) facilitates the opportunity to consider some of the important contextual influences inhabiting this world. With teachers at the centre, the 'micro-system' might be described as the daily interactions and relationships teachers have with pupils, support staff and parents. Into this micro-system, there are interactions from an outer 'meso-system' of influences from the wider school, directly and indirectly impacting upon the teacher, that junction point of thought, reflection and behaviour. The emotions experienced in response to micro- and meso-influences may be positive, for example, affirmation from colleagues, parents or community members that teachers are 'doing a good job'. Or they may be negative, perhaps from a stressful performance management observation. The 'exo-system' includes the wider influences of organizational bodies affecting practice, such as the Department for Education and the Office for Standards in Education (OfSTED). Over time, all contextual influences are present and can potentiate development but this relies on the teacher's ability to be aware of, and alert to, the micro- through to exo-factors shaping their practice and to be open-minded and willing to address assumptions (Brookfield, 1995; Dewey, 1933).

Window on research

Charteris, J. and Smith, J. (2017). 'Sacred and secret stories in professional knowledge landscapes: Learner agency in teacher professional learning', *Reflective Practice*, 18(5), pp. 600–12.

In the context of New Zealand, Charteris and Smith (2017, p. 609) examine how teachers engage in 'reflective practice that can support critical and collaborative practitioner research'. The qualitative enquiry reveals how teachers involved in a professional learning and development programme were assisted in developing their own enquires into practice. The paper examines the notion of learning as 'interrelational' between pupil, teacher and other professionals.

It uses a case study to reveal some of the tensions between 'sacred and secret' stories that a teacher might tell to describe their practice and it draws connections with the need for teachers to have 'space for agency' and 'trust' so that their practice is transformative.

The use of Brofenbrenner's (1979) model can be employed to examine the following example in practice that illustrates how the systems might be used to explore the emotional impact on teachers, parents and their children. The example focuses on an inspection of new premises in a rapidly expanding school, which found aspects of policy and procedural deficiencies. This led to further investigations by inspectors and what had been judged as an outstanding school was plunged into being publically rated as requiring improvement. This had significant emotional impact on the whole school community, with the possibility that the school might close unless things improved rapidly. Teaching staff appeared conflicted, with the worry of keeping their jobs, but continuing to teach, inspire and challenge pupils, under the scrutiny of inspection. As an independent provider of education, parents of children at the school had choice to remove their children and find alternative educational provision. In terms of Bronfenbrenner's (1979) Socio-ecological model, there was a tumbledown effect. The inspection process operating in the exo-system impacted upon the meso-system of the school and school community, which in turn impacted on the micro-system of the teacher, parents and children. Teachers experienced extreme conditions of 'emotional labor' (Hochschild, 1983): of being challenged emotionally to maintain practice as normal.

In order to manage their anxiety, the teachers generated a safe space (McCotter, 2001) to examine and reflect collectively (Eraut, 2002). They identified the need to exercise emotional intelligence, defined as the ability to recognize, understand and manage their emotions, as well as the ability to recognize, understand and influence the emotions of others (Goleman, 1995). Practically this meant being reflexive, identifying that the raw emotions being experienced were driving their behaviours. These were impacting upon others particularly other staff, pupils and their parents (both positively and negatively). After reflecting together, the teachers identified the need to create emotional balance by trying to have a positive outlook, being adaptable and embracing the changes around them. In effect, they became alert to the factors influencing their situations and practices – and their responsibility (as they saw it) to manage their reactions in order to develop a positive mindset and response to their everyday encounters.

A positive or growth mindset (Dweck, 2007) is the notion that intelligence is not fixed and that challenge is an opportunity to learn and improve abilities. The idea is that commitment and effort can create the conditions in which learning and resilience can manifest in accomplishment. There is not a pre-defined outcome of failure and despair but through being dedicated and resilient, teachers can influence and/or change outcomes. The suggestion is that teachers should not believe that they cannot do something, but that they just cannot do it yet. Demonstrating a growth mindset requires teachers to take responsibility for improving their situation, seeing setbacks as opportunities to learn, to actively seek new challenges, to persevere and to be action-oriented.

Reflective questions

1. Can you recall an experience in your professional practice where your emotions inhabited your reactions and responses, and influenced your behaviours?
2. What strategies did you use to make sense of your situation?
3. How was the situation resolved?

Reflexive questions

1. What did you learn through the process of reflection on this experience?
2. How might this have changed your subsequent behaviours?

Under extreme pressure, one teacher in the troubled school was action-oriented and successfully applied for a new role in another school. This appeared to be an apparent solution to their extreme anxiety. However, during the selection process and subsequent events, things changed dramatically. During several visits to the new school, experiencing the surroundings, teaching a lesson and meeting proposed new colleagues, the teacher felt a significant sense of loss, although this was rationalized as being in a new situation. A few days later the teacher met prospective parents at the troubled school to talk about teaching and classroom activities: engaging in the dynamics of the micro-system and revisiting the ethos and principles of the organization. The dialogue enabled reflection and reflexivity concerning the underlying values and beliefs that first attracted the teacher to the school. The teacher made the decision to stay, having acknowledged the significant impact their emotions played in their initial responses and actions to leave the unsettling and uncertain situation. Despite ongoing challenges the teacher demonstrated emotional resilience as the dynamic 'process or phenomenon of competence' which encompasses 'positive adaptation within the context of significant adversity' (Luther, Cicchetti and Becker, 2000, p. 554). Resilience in this context enabled a change to the locus of control from negativity into a solution-oriented approach. Subsequently, the troubled school reported that teacher relationships became stronger and ultimately the school was re-inspected with a positive outcome. The previous tumble-down effect, from exo-system through meso-system to micro-system, was reversed.

Implications for teachers

In this chapter, the terms 'reflection' and 'reflexivity' have been presented as the personal, social and emotional responsibilities of teachers. Some of the challenges and difficulties that teachers might experience have been explored but it has also been shown how these might be mitigated, so that teachers continue to demonstrate their expertise in managing and dealing with such complex and emotional aspects of practice. Teachers should consider how their responses and behaviours are affected by cultural, political, economical and social influences – acknowledging how historical biographies inhabit their practice and how they might become alert to their habitual and routine ways of working. This requires teachers to explore the unexplored and to develop skills of self-analysis through the uncomfortable.

Teachers may need to confront their strongly held beliefs and acknowledge that what they may have held to be true might need to change in light of new knowledge and/or experiences. Teachers might begin to reveal new ways of thinking as they understand that teaching and learning is neither fixed nor certain and is affected by a complexity of interrelated systems impacting upon practice (Bronfenbrenner, 1979). Both Dewey (1938) and Schön (1987) suggest that to be effective in practice requires professionals to consider the evidence of their work. Teachers should use reflection and reflexivity as the means to articulate not only what they do, but why and how they do it. Taking such an informed and conscious approach to systematic thinking enables teachers to be assured as to what might be affective in their current practice or what might need addressing.

Reflection and reflexivity provide the means of learning as teachers show consciousness in their thinking and a willingness to confront previously held values and beliefs. Referring to the previous analogy, teachers might learn to fold their arms in a different way! As Thomson and Pascal (2012, p. 319) state,

> We would wish to argue that a well-developed approach to reflective practice would incorporate both these elements, both the traditional notion of reflection as an analytical process and reflexive approaches with their emphasis on the mirroring of practice, and thereby undertaking a self-analysis.

Thompson and Pascal (2012) endorse the notion that reflection and reflexivity require teachers to unpick their own certainties, to modify thinking, to be adaptable and to develop the confidence to see things in different ways. However, as authors, we suggest that teachers also need perspective. Whilst acknowledging that knowledge and experiences are their own and are situated in unique, complex and ever-changing contexts (Brookfield, 1995), teachers also need to be supported by others. These may be those who can share experience and wisdom but who can also offer advice as teachers transform difficulties into challenges and challenges into positive actions. This involves emotional endeavour. Teachers need to be aware that responding with understanding to pupils, their parents and other professionals requires an awareness of factors inhabiting their environment (Bronfenbrenner, 1979).

There are many models of reflection that teachers may be aware of and also encouraged to follow but Finlayson (2015, p. 729) argues,

> There are no 'hard or fast' rules about what constitutes a reflective practice model nor is there a singular unified definition of reflection. This in itself suggests that reflective practice can be considered as a personal process, inferring that individuals can build a reflective model that works for them and the desired outcomes they wish to achieve.

Both Dewey (1938) and Schön (1987) advocate the need for professionals to consider the problems they encounter in practice not as mistakes but as interesting, fascinating curiosities to investigate. There is challenge for you, as the teacher, to be alert to your personal biographies and to engage in individual and collective reflection and reflexivity as the means to develop resilience and transform your practice.

Reflective questions

As a professional how do you engage with the core themes of this chapter:

1. that reflection is personal, influenced by what is known in the moment and, therefore, affects decisions concerning pupils (positively and negatively) and
2. that collective reflection is the means to develop resilience during challenging professional circumstances and/or situations.

Reflexive question

As a professional how do you engage with these core themes in relation to your own emotions and assumptions and biases?

Annotated bibliography

Dewey, J. (1933). *How we think: A restatement of the relation of reflective thinking to the educative process*. Boston, MA: Houghton Mifflin.

This is considered a seminal work that has strongly influenced subsequent developments in reflective practice over time. Dewey presents an accessible exploration of thinking and its relationship to learning through experience and interaction. He provides insights into the nature of thinking as a process that is distinct from the notion of thoughts.

Thompson, N. and Pascal, J. (2012). 'Developing critically reflective practice', *Reflective Practice*, 13(2), pp. 311–25.

Thompson and Pascal (2012, p. 311) present a paper that acknowledges reflective practice as an 'influential concept in various forms of professional education' but provides a critique of the oversimplification of reflection as used in practice. They provide a sociological perspective with the intention of ensuring that understandings of reflective practice are 'more theoretically sophisticated' (ibid.).

9

The Role of the Teacher

Ruth Wood and Claire Jackson,

with Sandra Bayliss and Nick Usher

Introduction

The teacher's role may be perceived and described in many ways. It is possible that emphasis is placed upon facilitating, supporting, leading and guiding the cognitive development of the learner. Skills, knowledge and understanding, which are embodied in curriculum documentation and presented according to subject relevance, are often foregrounded. The process of translating curricula such as this into practice is sufficiently challenging; however, the preceding chapters highlight the multi-faceted role of the teacher, which extends beyond the measureable and more tangible outcomes of learning. In an age of supercomplexity, the teacher is amidst competing and often conflicting demands, which are difficult to navigate. As a moral practice, teachers will consider and respond to the needs and well-being of the learner not only contemplating how pupils might perform in assessments but also reflecting upon the needs and experiences of the pupil as an individual in their own right – collaborating and communicating with other professionals beyond the geography of the classroom and forging sustainable and productive links between home and school. At the core of such activity are teachers' own values, and to gain a better understanding of these, this chapter examines the individual and the collective voice of teachers drawn from a range of practice settings. In so doing, this chapter explores the ways in which teachers conceptualize and enact their role and the factors that influence their values, identity and practice.

Being a teacher

Individual conversations with teachers in England during the 2017–18 academic year provided the basis for this chapter. In three instances, these were recorded and analysed in order to inform the discussion. Ten questions guided each conversation and provided a means of exploring the values, beliefs and experiences of teachers working in either an early years (for children from birth to five years of age) or primary setting (for pupils aged between seven and eleven years). As conversations, it was possible to explore ideas in a relatively informal manner where both individuals were able to consider, reflect upon and respond to one another's ideas and experiences. Each conversation was transcribed and analysed in order to identify some common themes and variations arising from individual circumstances. The contributors to the conversations have been included as authors, and have provided feedback in the development of this chapter.

The opening question designed to initiate the conversation, 'what is the role of a teacher?', may seem relatively straightforward; yet, responses varied quite widely and often included examples, which revealed some of the micro- and macro-activities alongside the range and diversity of roles within a role. Above all, the answers given by teachers highlighted the ever-present challenges and tensions, which require more than the verb 'teach' to adequately reflect all of the intricacies and complexities associated with this role. Initially, there was a tendency to list a range of terms, for example, the teacher is an 'educator', 'facilitator' or 'imparter of knowledge'. Alongside these terms there were a range of perceived responsibilities signalled using terms such as 'substitute parent', 'social worker', 'therapist' and 'carer'. Often, the list of terms was delivered with some humour, but then revised and modified to make distinctions between the teacher's role and that of others. For example, one teacher revised the use of the term 'therapist' and explained that 'I know that I am not a trained therapist but sometimes I feel as though I am providing some sort of therapy to parents or children because they can share their anxieties, worries and fears with you, as the teacher, and you need to be able to respond to them'.

Window on research

Löfström, E. and Poom-Valickis, K. (2013). 'Beliefs about teaching: Persistent or malleable? A longitudinal study of prospective student teachers' beliefs', *Teaching and Teacher Education*, 35, pp. 104–13.

Löfström and Poom-Valackis (2013) carried out a longitudinal study exploring the beliefs about the role of the teacher with Estonian undergraduates in their first and third years of a non-teaching degree programme. The driver for this research was concerned about the diminishing numbers of students entering teacher training. Students were asked to describe the role of a teacher using a metaphor and also to complete a knowledge-based instrument, which used rank ordering. The research questions were: (1) What metaphors do students use to express their beliefs about the teacher/teaching? (2) How do students' beliefs about the teacher's role (as measured with the teacher's knowledge-based instrument) differ between the first and the third years of study? (3) What kind of relationship exists between the measurement of beliefs using metaphors and the teacher's knowledge-based instrument in the first and third years of study? (4) Is there a difference in beliefs about the teacher's role between students who chose to enter teacher education programmes and those who chose other educational paths?

Analysis of the data identified that students in their first year most commonly used a metaphor that reflected the teacher as a nurturer or pedagogue, with others focusing on subject knowledge and didactic expertise. By the third year metaphors were often expanded to reflect a developing belief and understanding of teaching. The knowledge-based instrument produced similar findings with students who continued into teacher training scoring higher on the pedagogue element and lower on the subject matter expert element than those who did not choose teacher education. The researchers conclude from this that there is a dominating belief that the role of the teacher is that of a caretaker or someone who supports the upbringing and development of children.

When researching the beliefs of prospective practitioners in Estonia, Löfström and Poom-Valickis asked participants to offer metaphors that described the teacher (2013). For example, the participants completed the sentence 'A teacher is … ' with a wide variety of words and phrases including, but not restricted to, a leader, a second mother, a radio, a king (2013, p. 108). Overall, Löfström and Poom-Valickis's research highlighted the emphasis their participants placed primarily on the teacher as a 'nurturer' and thereafter on the importance of subject knowledge (2013, pp 111). This seems to echo the perspectives of the teachers in our study who shared specific examples from practice, which illustrated their perceptions of the conflicting demands between care and education aspects of the teacher's role. Similarly, the early years teacher identified the challenge of balancing the heart and the head (Cox and Sykes, 2016) when working with young children. She identified that an element of 'professional love' (Page, 2011) is required so that children feel secure in their environment and are ready to learn and develop.

During conversations, it became apparent that there exists an interplay between the terms 'role' and 'identity'. Roles are usually defined by the school or society and may be linked to a professional code of practice, whereas identities can be a source of meaning that is developed through individual experiences and reflections (Gu, 2014), often influenced by significant others. The interweaving of this terminology is evident in both the literature and the interviews with teachers. For example, when asked why they had entered the teaching profession, responses from teachers focused on 'making a difference in the lives of children and families'; 'enabling children to reach their potential'; and, in some way, 'impacting on a generation'. Pollard (2014) identifies similar attitudes, referring to them as 'early idealism'. Many teachers enter the profession with a strong sense of purpose and with a desire to contribute to communities and society. Personal values motivate them at the start of their teaching career and are drawn on as teachers find their place within schools and the profession. This brings challenges as teachers evaluate their practice within the context of a personal philosophy based on socially just practices alongside the statutory requirements of the profession.

As Moyles (2001, p. 90) states, 'For practice to reach professional status, both head and heart need to meet at the interface of reflection.' Whilst reflecting on their journey from newly qualified teachers to their current professional status, practitioners in this study identified changes that had taken place as they dealt with the daily struggles of practice related to pupils and policy. Drawing on past experiences and personal values, they looked towards their future image of self as a teacher. This refining process of development from initial teaching experiences to more confident professionalism is explored by Ewing and Manual (2005). They analyse the perceptions of new teachers through the stages of early expectations and a sense of vocation; early days of the first teaching appointment; early survival phase; finding a place; consolidating pedagogical content knowledge; and building a professional identity. One of the teachers in Ewing and Manual's study shared the views of our practitioners that the personal commitment and sacrifice required to meet their own high expectations of the professional role have impacted on their sense of self and identity.

Ewing and Manual (2005) conclude that the voice of the teacher needs to be heard more consistently through meaningful contexts within the infrastructure of the school. This can enable connections with other staff members and opportunities to reflect on personal philosophy, tensions, anxieties and successes within a co-constructive ethos. The personal values that underpin practice support this process of reflection and enable teachers to evaluate what they do in the classroom alongside what they believe about education and learning (see Chapter 8). This reflection also takes place within the context of external policy and curriculum challenges, highlighting another role of the teacher as a 'creative mediator of policy' (Pollard, 2014, p. 5). Our teachers identified that a strong sense of personal identity supported by considered values and beliefs also gave them the confidence, motivation and resilience to manage the balance between work and life, thus enabling them to more effectively provide high-quality learning experiences for each pupil and to maintain a positive sense of self and well-being. This can be viewed as a self-perpetuating cycle as these teachers then have the drive, enthusiasm and well-established personal philosophy to provide quality-learning opportunities for the pupils in their care.

Reflective question

Following Lostrom and Poom-Valickis's research, complete the sentence 'A teacher is …' with as many words or phrases as you can think of. How do these help to describe your values?

Reflexive question

What has shaped these values?

Drawing on values and beliefs can initiate an affective response, which then impacts on actions in the classroom and interactions with pupils, parents and colleagues (Hargreaves, 1998). It has already been recognized in this chapter that teachers are, most likely, driven by a need to protect and support their pupils and that they feel passionate about this role. Some contemporary research has concluded that such feelings and emotions are a necessary part of teaching (Claxton, 1999, Goleman, 1996) and highlights the importance of attuned teachers who see, hear, feel and sense 'the everyday nuances of children's lives' (Cox and Sykes, 2016, p. 16). There is, however, a complex interplay between care and education: another potential dilemma for the reflective teacher to engage with.

Cox and Sykes (2016) liken the role of the teacher to a kaleidoscope due to its ever-changing nature. This constant integration of status, identity and values is then subject to re-examination and testing within a societal context. During social change, the teacher can become a mediator 'bridging the past, the present and the future' (Gu, 2014, p. 4). For example, within assessment, the current government drive is focused on standardization, testing, raising levels of attainment and data; much of the resulting pedagogy is at odds with the philosophies of teachers who place the pupil at the centre of their practice and recognize the value of creativity within the curriculum. Many teachers are drawing on their professional values in order to navigate a way through this climate in order to provide inspiring and supportive ways of making a difference in the lives of pupils now and for the future. For example, curriculum-related teaching and management responsibilities such as after-school clubs, residential school trips, assemblies, lunchtime supervision and fundraising events including school fairs all lie outside the formal curriculum but are inevitably connected. These provide enhancements to the pupils' learning experience either directly or indirectly. Some would argue that as the curriculum becomes more focused upon reading, writing and mathematics, other subjects are pushed to the periphery and squeezed in terms of time and resources. The 'broad and balanced' curriculum advocated by the Schools Council (amongst others) in the 1970s has, perhaps, faced challenges with greater attention focused on what are referred to as 'core subjects', notably English and mathematics. In elevating some subject areas of the curriculum above others it might be argued that the cohesion and relatedness between subjects have been diminished with greater interest placed upon what pupils learn in a relatively diminished curriculum field. The OfSTED education inspection framework (2019) appears to be addressing the dilemma of balancing and interrelating subjects within the curriculum. Terminology such as 'well balanced, knowledge-rich, skills, and cultural capital' appears in the documentation and the impact of the framework on the role of the teacher will be interesting to monitor over time.

Reflective questions

1. What external influences do you think are constantly affecting your role as a teacher?
2. What tensions have you experienced in your role?

Reflexive questions

1. In what ways might these tensions affect your values?
2. Will they change or be affirmed?

It is impossible to separate the identity of the teacher from society. Drawing on Bronfenbrenner's (1979) ecological systems theory, teachers are able to recognize the external influences that shape their role. The pupils, the classroom environment, school policies and procedures, parents, colleagues, other professionals and government initiatives or changes impact upon the social and cultural construction of teacher identity. As Griffin (2008, p. 356) states, this formation of identity takes place at 'the intersection where the outside world meets the individual'.

Conflict, challenge and change

Inevitably, when exploring the range of activities undertaken by teachers, conversation turned towards some of the challenges, most notably tensions between a target-driven culture and the need to support pupils' development and well-being. Much has been written regarding performativity, new managerialism and neoliberal times; this chapter does not intend to revisit these debates but instead seeks to explore conflicting demands and the experiences of teachers in light of their professional values and beliefs. As revealed in the previous section, teachers placed the pupil's welfare and development at the core of their activity. Even when additional responsibilities were called upon such as the management of a curriculum area, the teachers described how their actions sought to enrich or support learning experiences.

Case study: Role conflict

Country: England

Age group: Seven to eleven years

Setting: Primary School

Participants involved: Primary school teacher

All teachers held additional roles and responsibilities. As a PE coordinator, one teacher disclosed how they invested evenings and weekends supporting pupils' participation at sporting events and how they were also responsible for the development of planning and assessment in the subject area. As they explained,

> You do it for the children. .... because you know that for some they would not have the opportunity to participate in activities if you didn't do it. It's a lot of extra work and it means you have less time to focus on planning for your own class, you know, marking their work and preparing for the next day. It's also not always seen by other people, as it is out of the school day and sometimes at weekends too. I mean I enjoy it because the children want to do it but it is hard to balance the two. When I've got reports to write it is almost impossible.

Outcomes Sometimes, additional roles and activities might resonate with one another, but in other instances they might compete and conflict with what might be considered to be the primary and perhaps most important role of the class teacher. As one teacher with management responsibilities stated, '... and teaching has to come in there somewhere. I love being in the classroom because I can actually be with the children and teach them something'.

What we can learn Even for those who were relatively new to the profession, some form of additional responsibility has been assigned. The teacher is effectively burdened with more responsibilities, which can only make it more challenging to focus on teaching-related activities in their expanding role. In management terms, this would be described as 'role-overload' and 'work overload' (Handy, 1993, p. 67) with additional tasks placed on top of or alongside the existing ones. It is during the conversations with teachers that the values they hold are revealed.

It is possible that teachers find their values challenged or displaced not only from increasing and potentially conflicting demands but also from the 'terrors of performativity' bringing about changes not only in the schools as organizations but also in each individual's understanding as to what it means to be a teacher (Ball, 2003, 2016). Among the various mechanisms of performativity and accountability, OfSTED inspections seemed to be particularly challenging with the period awaiting notification of an inspection described by one teacher as a time when 'you focus so much on the paperwork that you don't have time to do the job. I'm not saying that we let anything slide but we didn't necessarily do things in as timely a fashion as we did this time last year'. In such instances, teacher's values and beliefs are tested with the need to perform to the required standards sometimes running counter to the teachers' convictions. This apparent conflict raises discussion surrounding the need for teachers to 'employ some sort of moral compass' (Santry, 2018) in order to take a stand against perceived threats which do not appear to place the interests of the pupil at the heart of professional practice. In a competitive and performance-oriented system this is not without risk where perceptions of success (and failure) are often determined by measures, statistics and comparison. Uncertainty and self-doubt were visited and revisited in conversations with the teachers who raised their concerns and analysed their actions and specific events in an attempt to resolve what might be described as 'cognitive dissonance' (Festinger, 1962) where there are apparent inconsistencies between values and action. In such circumstances, individuals may change either their belief or their action. Changing belief is unlikely to be undertaken lightly or within a short space of time and so it is more likely that the action will cease or be subject to modification. However, where the latter incurs an element of risk resolution may involve adjusting perceptions associated with the action to justify or rationalize the conflict between belief and action.

In all conversations, the amount of paperwork involved in teaching was highlighted as being both necessary yet overwhelming with teachers seemingly trying to find some resolution to possible dissonance. Comments surrounding the collection and management of data, some of which are listed below, were particularly interesting and revealed some of the underlying tensions.

> '... there's lots and lots of paperwork ... recording everything you can although you may not need it ... but there may be that one instance when it is necessary and then you've got it.'
> ' ... the marking load is absolutely huge ... somewhere in there is the actual teaching and I love the teaching ... with everything else that goes on I would say I spend less than half of my time actually teaching ... face-to-face teaching.'
> ' ... taking into consideration all of the work I do outside the school day it's quite frightening how much of that time I actually spend teaching the children.'

Perhaps unsurprisingly, all of the teachers indicated that their working week would almost always extend into evenings and weekends, a trend which was noted by Campbell and Neill in 1994 and which remains pertinent in a recent study commissioned by the DfE, which reported that of 3,186 teachers completing an online survey, one-quarter of full-time teachers and nearly one-third of part-time teachers undertook work outside the school hours (DfE, 2017, p. 3). According to the Department for Education's workload challenge survey, there were two tasks that were most cited as unnecessarily contributing to workload. These were 'recording, inputting, monitoring and analysing data (56%)' and 'excessive/depth of marking – detail and frequency required (53%)' (DfE, 2015, pp. 7–8). Respondents indicated that both of these were exacerbated by 'accountability/perceived pressures of Ofsted (53%)' and 'tasks set by senior/middle leaders (51%)' (DfE, 2015, p. 8). The National Federation for Educational Research (NFER) analysed survey responses from 'at least 1000 primary and secondary school teachers' undertaken at three intervals over one year and twenty-one interviews of teachers who were considering or who had already left a teaching career in the state sector (Lynch et al., 2016, pp. 21–4). The analysis of these data supports the findings from the DfE workload challenge survey and suggests that inspection and changes in policy are perceived by teachers as critical factors in increasing workload.

It is possible that more experienced teachers require less time to plan for and assess learning as they can draw upon a knowledge base informed by their practice. This was mentioned by one of the teachers; however, there is also a sense that this, in addition to an increasing array of middle management roles, may result in the proliferation of paperwork and procedures. Recruitment and retention of teachers have also been revealed as problematic with teacher numbers continuing to fall at a time when there are increasing numbers of pupils (Foster, 2018, p. 4). Concerns regarding teacher retention and rates of attrition also seem to exist in other countries (Geiger and Pivovarova, 2018; Schaefer, Long and Clandinin, 2012).

Schaefer, Long and Clandinin (2012) have undertaken an extensive literature review drawing on research conducted across the globe and they arrive at the conclusion that there is a 'need to shift the dialogue from the focus on retaining teachers towards a conversation about sustaining teachers throughout their careers' (2012, p. 118). Using a mixed method approach involving 1,400 teachers from thirty-seven Arizona public schools from 2011 to 2014, Geiger and Pivovarova (2018) also argue that improved 'positive working conditions, teacher involvement, and providing teachers with opportunities for professional development' were key elements to improving teacher retention (2018, p. 619). Issues that have been identified through discussion with education professionals in preparation for this chapter also illustrate how teachers might become morally disillusioned and overloaded with the pressures of paperwork and targets. As this situation reaches a crisis point in England, the Government appears to be formally tackling workload through the Ofsted education inspection framework (2019) along with reduced workload documentation and tool kits (DfE, 2019a). These measures are welcomed by educators but will require time to embed and have a measurable impact.

Fundamentally, all of the interviewed teachers reiterated that making a difference to pupils' lives through creating positive learning experiences, supporting their overall development and their well-being was what brought them into teaching and was what they found most rewarding. It was this, alongside the values and support shared and provided with and between their colleagues, which effectively countered the challenges they faced. They recognized the relevance of assessment and record-keeping in order to gain a clear understanding of individual pupil's needs and to support progression but these comments were tempered by concerns which signalled perceived inconsistencies regarding what they believed to be the teacher's role and the demands made upon them in practice. Certainly, the discussions with teachers highlighted the many demands associated with accountability and performativity measures with assessing, marking and monitoring dominating conversations. There were anxieties surrounding the intensified use of data, its expansion within the education sector and the challenges and tensions of data-driven practice. Roberts-Holmes argues that the demands placed on teachers to produce 'appropriate data' only serve to diminish and narrow the focus of early years teaching (2014, p. 303); effectively, this would mean that the measurable and the measured become the priority – this, at a time when the production and availability of data through technological developments is vastly accelerating and multiplying.

In what has been described as 'the information society' (Webster, 2006), or in earlier literature as 'the knowledge society' (Hargreaves, 2003) and 'the knowledge-based economy' (Organisation for Economic Cooperation and Development, 1996), the speed, capacity and arrangement of technology in a vast array of networks upon networks bring about a sense of instability and uncertainty. With attention placed upon economics, productivity and employability, the teacher is tasked with preparing pupils to live and flourish in this fast-paced climate of change where 'innovation, flexibility and commitment to change' are essential for economic prosperity (Hargreaves, 2003, p. 1). The digital revolution and technological change impact upon our understanding of who you are and how you act in what Barnett describes as a 'supercomplex world' (Barnett, 2000, p. 257). Teachers face challenges in finding an understanding of their roles often with a sense that the problems faced by society in a time of supercomplexity can only be resolved by the actions of the teacher. This, perhaps, has always been the case with education seen as a means of resolving society's problems. In the knowledge society, the teacher is required to not only prepare the workforce of the future, acting as 'catalyst' in forging a successful future, but also counter the vast and wide-ranging problems within such a society all of which are undertaken against a backdrop of performativity where high expectations generate the potential for teachers to become 'casualties'. Hargreaves presents this as 'the knowledge society triangle' where the teacher is placed centrally in a 'triangle of competing interests and imperatives' (2003, pp. 10–11). It is useful to contemplate the potential tensions created by such demands; yet, arguably, the values and principles of the teacher in terms of pupils' development might be viewed as a critical element in navigating this challenging terrain.

Reflective question

As a teacher, how might you seek to resolve some of the challenges you face, acting as a catalyst or counterpoint rather than a casualty?

Resolving the conflict

In contrast to Hargreaves's knowledge society triangle, Moyles's 'black hole model of early years practitioners' focuses upon their emotional commitment to supporting young children's development (2001, p. 88). In highlighting the perceived powerlessness and vulnerability of early years practitioners, Moyles offers a model which contains a 'black hole' signifying the pressures from a range of sources effectively nullifying a practitioner's emotional drive to adhere to their values and principles. Although focusing upon early years practitioners, the model could easily translate to other sectors where confidence in practice is diminished through an array of demands and expectations – what Hargreaves might refer to as being a casualty.

Teachers are finding themselves facing ideological tensions as they try to balance their knowledge and experience of how pupils learn and develop with the conflicting demands of curricula and assessment procedures. Bradbury and Roberts-Holmes (2018) recognize that there has traditionally been a mismatch between the values and beliefs of the teacher and policymakers; however, the gap appears to be widening as social-constructivist pedagogy in the classroom clashes with the positivist method of assessment and performativity. As one early years teacher stated, 'I felt frustrated as I tried to meet the requirements of a data-driven climate and stay true to my philosophy of how children learn best which is underpinned by personal values, theory and reflection.'

Research and theory have identified that young children have a natural exuberance and curiosity for life and that deep-level learning and development takes place when they are able to construct meaning of the world both independently and in collaboration with others (Edwards et al., 1998; Vygostky, 1978). Real learning occurs when they are actively involved: building on prior learning and constructing knowledge (Piaget, 1929). This philosophy of child development underpins the Early Years Foundation Stage (EYFS) (DfE, 2017), as well as proposals for a reformed framework (DfE, 2019), with its play-based, child-centred pedagogy and assessment through observation; yet, early years practitioners are faced with the dilemmas associated with the proposed introduction of the reception baseline assessment (RBA) – a process that collects numerical data in the areas of maths, language, communication and literacy as a starting point for measuring pupil progress within schools. The RBA should take place within the first six weeks of the child starting school at the age of four. This is an important time when young children are in a state of transition and should be building social relationships that provide the foundation for all learning (Broadhead and Burt, 2012). The RBA is in direct contrast to socio-cultural pedagogy and the principles of the EYFS itself and could cause ideological conflict for teachers as they consider their role as carer alongside that of a collector of 'high stakes' data (Bradbury and Holmes, 2018, p. 22). Wyse and Torrance (2009, p. 224) claim that this pressure on teachers is 'driving teaching in exactly the opposite direction to that which other research indicates will improve teaching, learning and attainment'. The teacher's sense of professionalism is challenged and at times undermined as they try to stay true to their values and meet the requirements placed on the school by measures of performativity and accountability.

> In the early years team we sometimes feel like lone voices within the school battling against imposed teaching and learning styles. Staff meetings can become battlegrounds as we fight for what we believe is best for children; shouldn't the children be our focus after all? (EY teacher)

Moyles and Adams (2001) concluded that this feeling of disempowerment reduced the vocational passion of the teachers in their Statements of Entitlement to Play (StEPs) project, causing them to sink into 'the black hole'. However, before teachers reach the point of no return, 'pedagogical magic' can take place 'that keeps the romance of teaching alive for great teachers' (Steinberg and Kincheloe, 1998, p. 228). When there is an interweaving of passion, reflective practice, intellect and negotiation teachers can begin to navigate the complexities of performativity and children's learning and development.

When researching Early Childhood Education and Care (ECEC) in areas of high poverty within Australia, Skattebol, Adamson and Woodrow (2016) allow the voices of practitioners to reveal the depth and detail of their practice. Beyond the performativity agenda, the accounts from practitioners refer to the importance of knowledge and understanding in child development and pedagogy. More than this, however, it is the application of this knowledge in context: recognizing and critically reflecting upon the socio-cultural, political and economical landscape to address the needs of pupils and their families in order to negotiate and secure a socially just outcome.

Window on research

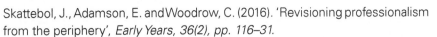

Skattebol, J., Adamson, E. and Woodrow, C. (2016). 'Revisioning professionalism from the periphery', *Early Years, 36(2), pp. 116–31.*

This study presents an insight into the perspectives of those working in early childhood education and care with regard to professionalism and professional identity. The periphery is described as 'contexts of high poverty', which 'are frequently located on the periphery, sometimes geographically but always economically, socially and politically'. One of the main purposes of the research is to allow those living and working in such circumstances to have a voice.

A mixed methods research design was employed with qualitative data from semi-structured interviews alongside quantitative data mapping the demographics of a neighbourhood. Overall, the researchers collected interview data from 'six sites across four Australian states', each of which was selected from the analysis of the demographic data. This article reports on the interviews undertaken with service providers alongside other 'key informants' in order to understand practitioners' perceptions with regard to their role and practice.

The analysis of the interviews with service providers revealed three main competency-related themes, namely: rationality, emotionality and criticality. Referring to earlier research conducted by individuals such as Moyles (2001) and Osgood (2010), Skattebol, Adamson and Woodrow, the researchers, highlighted practitioners' views of the affective and emotional as being 'front and centre' to their role. More than this, the researchers revealed that the emotional was also tempered with a critical understanding of each family's context from a political, economical and sociological perspective. Beyond regulatory frameworks and standards, practitioners indicated the need to rationally identify and address the complex challenges faced by the families; drawing upon knowledge and understanding of child development and pedagogy.

Skattebol, Adamson and Woodrow (2016) concluded that the combination of criticality, emotionality and rationality was important in the work of the practitioners. The interviews also revealed the need for flexibility in their approach, an alertness to the funding streams and policy context, an ability to be 'emotionally critical' to the circumstances and needs of the families and to possess rational skills associated with child development and pedagogy. Reaching beyond what they refer to as the 'education/care dichotomy', they argue that for those working at the periphery, 'ethical entrepreneurialism is at the core of everyday practice'.

Implications for teachers

Although tensions are ever-present and the landscape of education is subject to a variety of challenges, the voices of teachers from existing research and within this chapter reveal the ways in which they navigate the tensions arising from this turbulence. There is evidence that teachers mediate between the demands, expectations and needs associated with a wide range of individuals; act as counterpoints to a fast-paced technologically oriented world; and address perceived imbalances created by economical and political demands.

Values and beliefs are critical and influential components to a teacher's practice and these are informed by their knowledge and understanding of child development. Critical awareness and reflection on practice in a given context contribute to the ways in which theory informs and is informed by action. Essentially, the education professional adopts a caring and nurturing approach but this alone does not define the complex and harder-to-capture role of the teacher. This was evidenced in the interviews of the teachers who demonstrated awareness of the tensions and demands inherent in their role, maintaining a sense of moral purpose and a desire to contribute to society. In particular, their sense of responsibility to pupil's welfare and learning appears to have a significant influence on their ever-evolving professional identity and conduct.

Recognizing that identity is subject to change with values and beliefs challenged through dilemmas brought about by a changing social and political climate within education, it is possible that teachers can experience 'identity dissonance' (Pillen, Den Brock and Beijard, 2013, p. 86) resulting in internal conflict between their personal and professional values. Teacher autonomy in the decision making of practice may be challenged, for example, when they struggle to adhere to what they believe and, at the same time, attempt to meet measures of performativity. In such circumstances, self-confidence and creativity may diminish as a teacher's judgement is questioned – potentially leading to a compliant workforce that is risk averse and without an influencing voice (Sachs, 2016). In acknowledging this, the need to strengthen teachers' understanding of professional knowledge and their sense of professionalism might also increase the confidence of teachers in making their voice heard. This might alleviate the pressures that they experience on a daily basis and not only enable them to mediate, manage and resolve the many challenges that they face, but perhaps address and counteract that which causes such pressures. Continuing Professional Development (CPD) that challenges intellectual thinking and fosters self-awareness has the potential to transform professional identity, thereby enabling teachers to navigate their way around the 'knowledge society triangle' (Hargreaves, 2003). As highlighted by Moyles and Adams, teachers may already have diminished confidence and feel that they are in the 'black hole' (2001); however, current research (Sachs, 2016) and the voices of teachers involved in the interviews within this chapter indicate that positive action can be taken in order to tackle the current dilemmas and tensions within the profession.

An alternative definition of the role of the teacher is 'researcher'. In recent years 'research-led practice' and 'evidence-based practice' have been promoted and evaluated through government documentation, with the aim of developing an ethos of continual reflection and improvement in schools (Coldwell et al., 2017; GTC, 2006; Walker et al., 2019). Through CPD, some senior managers and teachers have aimed to develop a learning community that openly discusses and questions practice-related research, and, where appropriate, draws on school- or classroom-based evidence to inform new and existing initiatives. Through this medium it would be possible to challenge key issues such as datafication, workload and the general mismatch between government policies and teachers' pedagogical values. Dahlberg et al. (2013, p. 35) state that the education system is 'fragile and open to challenge'. A research literate community of teachers could redress the balance: reverting to a self-confident, adventurous team of professionals who create innovative curricula and pedagogies (BERA, 2014; p. 23, Sachs, 2016).

Teachers, as lifelong learners and with the desire to keep pupils at the centre of their practice, can be agents of change. They can question and challenge procedures and initiatives that contradict their professional values and pedagogical understanding of how pupils learn and develop. Debate around the key issues summarized in this chapter should be encouraged and enabled so that teachers continue to feel empowered and motivated to develop best practice in their classrooms and cultivate a stronger sense of what it is to be a teacher professional.

Reflective questions

As a professional how do you engage with the core themes of this chapter?

1. that teachers enact practice having to navigate tensions that exist and
2. that teachers as 'researchers' might influence positive change.

Reflexive question

As a professional how do you engage with these core themes in relation to your own emotions and assumptions and biases?

Annotated bibliography

Biesta, G., Priestley, M. and Robinson, S. (2015). 'The role of beliefs in teacher agency', *Teachers and Teaching*, 21(6), pp. 624–40.

Biesta et al. report on a two-year study that focuses upon teachers' beliefs. From an individual and collective perspective, the researchers examine the discourse, which affects the ways in which teachers take action during policy implementation within Scotland. The research reveals the apparent disconnect between the individual and the collective and argues that for teacher agency to be effective, a shared professional vision needs to be developed.

Cox, A. and Sykes, G. (2016). *The multiple identities of the reception teacher pedagogy and purpose*. London: Sage.

This book recognizes the emotional connection that reception teachers have to their work and does not seek to separate education from care. It explores the multiple roles undertaken by the practitioner with chapters examining a wide range of topics including child development, the teacher as a researcher and early childhood education.

Bibliography

Chapter 1 Setting the Context

Ball, S. J. (2008). *The education debate*. Bristol: Policy Press.

Bowlby, J. (1958). 'The nature of a child's tie to his mother'. *International Journal of Psychoanalysis*, 39, pp. 350–73.

Campbell-Barr, V. (2009). 'Contextual issues in assessing value for money in early years education', *National Institute Economic Review*, 207(1), pp. 90–101.

Charlesworth, R. (2017). *Understanding child development*. 10th edn. Boston, MA: Cengage Learning.

Lubeck, S. (1998). 'Is DAP for everyone?', *Childhood Education*, 74(5), pp. 283–92.

Parker-Rees, R. (2015). 'Concepts of childhood: Meeting with difference', in Parker-Rees, R. and Leeson, C. (eds.) *Early childhood studies: An introduction to the study of children's lives and children's worlds*. 4th edn. London: Sage, pp. 191–203.

Penn, H. (2012b). 'Shaping the future: How human capital arguments about investment in early childhood are being (mis)used in poor countries', in Yelland, N. (ed.) *Contemporary perspective on early childhood education*. Maidenhead: Open University Press, pp. 49–65.

Piaget, J. (1936) *The origin of intelligence in the child*. London: Routledge and Kegan Paul.

Skinner, B. F. (1957). *Verbal behaviour*. New York: Appleton-Century-Crofts.

Smidt, S. (2013). *The Developing child in the 21st century: A global perspective on child development*. 2nd edn. London: Routledge.

Chapter 2 The Professional Self

Bernstein, B. (1999). 'Vertical and horizontal discourse: An essay', *British Journal of Sociology of Education*, 20(2), pp. 157–73.

Bernstein, B. B. (2000). *Pedagogy, symbolic control, and identity: Theory, research, critique*. Revised edn. Oxford: Rowman and Littlefield.

Biesta, G. (2014). 'Pragmatising the curriculum: Bringing knowledge back into the curriculum conversation, but via pragmatism', *The Curriculum Journal*, 25(1), pp. 29–49.

Bogatić, K., Visnjic Jevtic, A., Campbell-Barr, V. and Georgeson, J. (2018). *Initial literature review – Interpreting child-centredness to support quality and diversity in early childhood education and care*. Plymouth: University of Plymouth. Available at: https://www.plymouth.ac.uk/research/child-centred-diversity-in-quality-early-childhood-education-and-care.

Cameron, C. and Millar, J. (2016). 'The early years professional in England', in Vandenbroeck, M., Urban, M. and Peeters, J. (eds.) *Pathways to professionalism in early childhood education and care.* London: Rutledge, pp. 103–18.

Campbell-Barr, V. (2019a). *Professional knowledge and skills in the early years.* London: Sage.

Campbell-Barr, V. (2019b). 'Professional knowledges for early childhood education and care', *Journal of Childhood Studies*, 44(1), pp. 134–46.

Furlong, J. and Whitty, G. (2017). 'Knowledge traditions in the study of education', in Whitty, G. and Furlong, J. (eds.) *Knowledge and the study of education: An international exploration.* Oxford: Symposium Books, pp. 13–60.

Georgeson, J. and Payler, J. (2014). 'Qualifications and quality in the early years foundation stage', in Moyles, J., Payler, J. and Georgeson, J. (eds.) *Early years foundations.* Maindenhead: McGraw Hill Education, pp. 52–64.

Hordern, J. (2017). 'Bernstein's sociology of knowledge and education(al) studies', in Furlong, J. and Whitty, G. (eds.) *Knowledge and the study of educaion: An international exploration.* Oxford: Symposium Books, pp. 191-210.

Jensen, J. J. (2016). 'The Danish pedagogue education', in Vandenbroeck, M., Urban, M. and Peeters, J. (eds.) *Pathways to professionalism in early childhood education and care* Oxon: Routledge, pp. 15–28.

Johnson, D. (2000). *Intuition, culture and the development of academic literacy. The intuitive practioner.* Buckingham: Open University Press.

Moss, P. (2006). 'Farewell to childcare?', *National Institute Economic Review*, 195(1), pp. 70–83.

Nutbrown, C. and Clough, P. (2014). *Early childhood education: History, philosophy and experience.* Nutbrown, C. and Clough, P. (eds.) 2nd edn. London: Sage.

Oberhuemer, P., Schreyer, I. and Neuman, M. (2010). *Professionals in early childhood education and care systems: European profiles and perspectives.* Leverkusen Opladen: Barbra Budich Publishers.

Rhedding-Jones, J. (2005). 'Decentering Anglo-American curricular power in early childhood education: Learning, culture, and "child development" in higher education coursework', *Journal of Curriculum Theorizing*, 21(3), pp. 143–65.

Urban, M., Vandenbroek, M., Lazzari, A., Peeters, J. and van Laere, K. (2011). *Competence requirements in early childhood education and care (CoRe).* London and Ghent: University of East London, University of Ghent and European Commission Directorate-General for Education and Culture. Available at: https://download.ei-ie.org/Docs/WebDepot/CoReResearchDocuments2011.pdf.

Winch, C. (2004). *Philosophy and educational policy: A critical introduction.* London: RoutledgeFalmer.

Winch, C. (2014). 'Know-how and knowledge in the professional curriculum', in Young, M. and Muller, J. (eds.) *Knowledge, expertise and the professions.* London: Routledge, pp. 47–60.

Young, M. (2007). *Bringing knowledge back In: From social constructivism to social realism in the sociology of education by young.* Oxon: Routledge.

Young, M. and Muller, J. (2007). 'Truth and truthfulness in the sociology of educational knowledge', *Theory and Research in Education*, 5(2), pp. 173–201.

Young, M. and Muller, J. (2014). 'From the sociology of professions to the sociology of professional knowledge', in Young, M. and Muller, J. (eds.) *Knowledge, expertise and the professions.* London: Routledge, pp. 3–17.

Chapter 3 The Need for Health and Well-Being

Archer, T. (2014). 'Health benefits of physical exercise for children and adolescents', *Journal of Novel Physiotherapies*, 4(2), pp. 1–4.

Baker, C. (2018). *Obesity statistics.* Available at: file:///C:/Users/ku34169/Downloads/SN03336%20(2).pdf.

Bellfield, C., Farquharson, C. and Sibieta, L. (2018). *2018 annual report on education spending in England.* Available at: https://www.ifs.org.uk/uploads/publications/comms/R150.pdf.

Bento, G. and Dias, G. (2017). 'The importance of play for young children's health and development', *Porto Biomedical Journal*, 2(5), pp. 157–60.

Blössner, M. (2009). 'School health, nutrition and education for all: Levelling the playing field', *Bulletin of the World Health Organisation*, 87(1), p. 75.

Bousted, M. (2018). *Comment on IFS report of school funding.* Available at: https://neu.org.uk/latest/comment-ifs-report-school-funding.

Bower, J. M. and Carroll, A. (2017). 'Capturing real-time emotional states and triggers for teachers through the teacher wellbeing web-based application t*: A pilot study', *Teaching and Teacher Education*, 65, pp. 183–91.

Britton, J., Farquhason, C. and Sibieta, L. (2019). *2019 annual report on education spending in England.* Available at: https://www.ifs.org.uk/publications/14369.

Bronfenbrenner, U. (1992) *Ecological systems theory.* London: Jessica Kingsley.

Crenna-Jennings, W. (2018). *Vulnerable children and social care in England: A review of the evidence.* Available at: https://epi.org.uk/publications-and-research/vulnerable-children-and-social-care-in-england/.

Crown copyright (2017). *The Scottish health survey 2016.* Available at: https://www.gov.scot/Resource/0052/00525472.pdf.

Department for Education and Department of Health (2015). *The special educational needs and disability code of practice.* Available at: https://assets.publishing.service.gov.uk/government/uploads/system/uploads/attachment_data/file/398815/SEND_Code_of_Practice_January_2015.pdf.

Department of Health (2017). *Health survey (NI) first results 2016/17.* Available at: https://www.health-ni.gov.uk/sites/default/files/publications/health/hsni-first-results-16-17.pdf.

Department of Health and Social Care (2019). *UK Chief Medical Officers' Physical Activity Guidelines.* Available at: https://assets.publishing.service.gov.uk/government/uploads/system/uploads/attachment_data/file/832868/uk-chief-medical-officers-physical-activity-guidelines.pdf (accessed 28 September 2020).

DfE (2011). *Teachers' standards: Guidance for school leaders, school staff and governing bodies.* Available at: https://www.gov.uk/government/uploads/system/uploads/attachment_data/file/665520/Teachers__Standards.pdf.

DfE (2013a). *Science programmes of study: key stages 1 and 2.* Available at: https://assets.publishing.service.gov.uk/government/uploads/system/uploads/attachment_data/file/425618/PRIMARY_national_curriculum_-_Science.pdf. (accessed 30 August 2018).

DfE (2013b). *Evidence on physical education and sport in schools.* Available at: https://assets.publishing.service.gov.uk/government/uploads/system/uploads/attachment_data/file/226505/Evidence_on_physical_education_and_sport_in_schools.pdf.

DfE (2013c). *Evidence on physical education and sport in schools.* Available at: https://assets.publishing.service.gov.uk/government/uploads/system/uploads/attachment_data/file/226505/Evidence_on_physical_education_and_sport_in_schools.pdf. (accessed 30 August 2018).

DfE (2014a). *National curriculum in England: framework for key stages 1 to 4.* Available at: https://www.gov.uk/government/publications/national-curriculum-in-england-framework-for-key-stages-1-to-4/the-national-curriculum-in-england-framework-for-key-stages-1-to-4 (accessed 21 October 2019).

DfE (2017a). *Statutory framework for the early years foundation stage. Setting the standards for learning, development and care for children from birth to five.* Available at: https://www.foundationyears.org.uk/files/2017/03/EYFS_STATUTORY_FRAMEWORK_2017.pdf.

DfE (2017b). *Statutory framework for the early years foundation stage. Setting the standards for learning, development and care for children from birth to five.* Available at: https://www.foundationyears.org.uk/files/2017/03/EYFS_STATUTORY_FRAMEWORK_2017.pdf (accessed 21 October 2019).

DfE (2018). *Working together to Safeguard children.* Available at: https://assets.publishing.service.gov.uk/government/uploads/system/uploads/attachment_data/file/729914/Working_Together_to_Safeguard_Children-2018.pdf.

Dobbs-Oates, J. and Morris, C. W. (2014). 'The case for interprofessional education in teacher education and beyond', *Journal of Education for Teaching*, 42(1), pp. 50–65.

Donnelly, L. (2014). 'Lord Coe: Lazy lifestyles will shorten our children's lives', *The Telegraph*, 8 April. Available at: https://www.telegraph.co.uk/news/health/news/10750433/Lord-Coe-Lazy-lifestyles-will-shorten-our-childrens-lives.html.

Earle, J. (2016). *Children and young people's mental health.* British Medical Association. Available at: https://www.bma.org.uk/media/2055/guuk-2016-progress-report-mental-health-earle.pdf.

Education Support Partnership (2017). *Health Survey 2017.* Available at: https://www.educationsupportpartnership.org.uk/sites/default/files/education_staff_health_survey_2017.pdf.

Field, T. (2012). 'Exercise research on children and adolescents', *Complementary Therapies in Clinical Practice*, 18(1), pp. 54–9.

Forsey, A. (2017). *Hungry holidays*. Available at: http://www.frankfield.co.uk/upload/docs/Hungry%20Holidays.pdf.

Frith, E. (2016). *CentreForum commission on children and young people's mental health: State of the nation*. Available at: https://epi.org.uk/wp-content/uploads/2018/01/State-of-the-Nation-report-web.pdf.

Hall, E., Chai, W. and Albrecht, J. (2017). 'Phenomenology of classroom teachers' experience with nutrition education', *Journal of Nutrition Education and Behavior*, 49(7), S63–4.

Harrist, A. W., Topham, G. L., Hubbs-Tait, L., Shriver, L. H. and Swindle, T. M. (2017). 'Psychosocial factors in children's obesity: Examples from an innovative line of inquiry', *Child Development Perspectives*, 11(4), pp. 275–81.

Health and Safety at Work Act (1974). Available at: http://www.legislation.gov.uk/uksi/1974/1439/contents/made.

Herman, K. C., Hickmon-Rosa, J. and Reinke, W. M. (2018). 'Empirically derived profiles of teacher stress, burnout, self-efficacy, and coping and associated student outcomes', *Journal of Positive Behavior Interventions*, 20(2), pp. 90–100.

Ingle, H. and Coan, S. (2017). *We asked children why they don't get enough exercise – Here's what they said*. Available at: http://theconversation.com/we-asked-children-why-they-dont-get-enough-exercise-heres-what-they-said-74272.

Jones, W. H. S. (1931). *Hippocrates volume VI*. Cambridge, MA: Harvard University Press.

Jourdan, D. (2011) *Health Education in Schools. The challenge of teacher training*. Saint-Denis, France; Inpes Coll. Sante en action.

Jukes, M. C. H., Drake, L. J. and Bundy, D. A. P. (2007) *School health, nutrition and education for all: Levelling the playing field*. Wallington: CABI Publishing.

Kyttälä, P., Erkkola, M., Lehtinen-Jacks, S., Ovaskainen, M., Uusitalo, L., Veijola, R., Simell, O., Knip, M. and Virtanen, S. (2014). 'Finnish Children Healthy Eating Index (FCHEI) and its associations with family and child characteristics in pre-school children', *Public Health Nutrition*, 17(11), pp. 2519–27.

Launer, J. (2018). 'The irresistible rise of interprofessional supervision', *Postgraduate Medical Journal*, 94(1114), pp. 481–2.

Lewis, I. and Lenehan, C. (2014). *Children and young people's health outcomes annual report 2013 to 2014*. Available at: https://assets.publishing.service.gov.uk/government/uploads/system/uploads/attachment_data/file/307011/CYPHOF_Annual_Report_201314_FORMAT_V1.5.pdf.

Mackareth, C. J., Brown, J. S., Learmonth, A. M. and Ashton, J. R. (2014). *Promoting public mental health and well-being: Principles into practice*. London: Jessica Kingsley Publishers.

Management of Health and Safety at Work Regulations (1999). Available at: http://www.legislation.gov.uk/uksi/1999/3242/contents/made.

Marmot, M. (2010). *Fair society, healthy lives*. Available at: http://www.instituteofhealthequity.org/resources-reports/fair-society-healthy-lives-the-marmot-review/fair-society-healthy-lives-full-report-pdf.pdf.

McLean, L., Abry, T., Taylor, M., Jimenez, M. and Granger, K. (2017). 'Teachers' mental health and perceptions of school climate across the transition from training to teaching', *Teaching and Teacher Education*, 65, pp. 230–40.

Mental Health Foundation (2018). *Children and young people.* Available at: https://www. mentalhealth.org.uk/a-to-z/c/children-and-young-people.

Nader, P. R., Bradley, R. H., Houts, R. M., McRitchie, S. L. and O'Brien, M. (2008). 'Moderate-to-vigorous physical activity from ages 9 to 15 years', *Journal of the American Medical Association*, 300(3), pp. 295–305.

Digital, N. H. S. (2017). *National child measurement programme.* Available at: https:// digital.nhs.uk/data-and-information/publications/statistical/national-child-measurement-programme/2016-17-school-year.

Digital, N. H. S. (2018). *Mental health of children and young people in England 2017.* Available at: https://files.digital.nhs.uk/A0/273EE3/MHCYP%202017%20Trends%20 Characteristics.pdf.

Nikiforidou, Z. (2017). '"It is riskier": Preschoolers' reasoning of risky situations', *European Early Childhood Education Research Journal*, 25(4), pp. 612–23.

Ofsted (2013). *Not enough physical in physical education.* Available at: https://www.gov. uk/government/news/not-enough-physical-in-physical-education.

Ofsted (2018). *Obesity, healthy eating and physical activity in primary schools.* Available at: https://assets.publishing.service.gov.uk/government/uploads/system/uploads/ attachment_data/file/726114/Obesity__healthy_eating_and_physical_activity_in_ primary_schools_170718.pdf.

Parsons, T. (1951). *The Social System.* London: Routledge and Kegan Paul.

Paterson, A. and Grantham, R. (2016). 'How to make teachers happy: An exploration of teacher wellbeing in the primary school context', *Educational and Child Psychology*, 33(2), pp. 90–102.

Public Health England (2014). *The link between pupil health and wellbeing and attainment. A briefing for head teachers, governors and staff in education settings.* Available at: https://www.gov.uk/government/publications/the-link-between-pupil-health-and-wellbeing-and-attainment.

Public Health England (2017). *Health matters: Obesity and the food environment.* Available at: https://www.gov.uk/government/publications/health-matters-obesity-and-the-food-environment/health-matters-obesity-and-the-food-environment–2.

Reid, H., Westergaard, J. and Claringbull, N. (2013). *Effective supervision for counsellors.* London: Learning Matters.

Rhee, K. E., McEachern, R. and Jilalian, E. (2014). 'Parent readiness to change differs for overweight dietary and physical activity behaviours', *Journal of the Academy of Nutrition and Dietetics*, 114(10), pp. 1601–10.

Roth, A., Goldsworthy, N., Folkens, S. and Edens, N. (2017). 'Small bites, big change! Teacher facilitated nutrition program increases healthy eating knowledge and vegetable consumption', *Journal of Nutrition Education and Behavior*, 49(7), pp. S78–9.

Schoenfeld, T. J., Rada, P., Pieruzzini, P. R., Hsueh, B. and Gould, H. (2011). 'Physical exercise prevents stress-induced activation of the granule neurons and enhances local inhibitory mechanisms in the dentate gyrus', *Journal of Neuroscience*, 33(18), pp. 7770–7.

Slottje, D., Tchernis, R., Baltagi, B. and Sadka, E. (2015). *Current issues in health economics.* Bingley: Emerald Publishing Ltd.

Su, J., Wu, Z. and Su, Y. (2018). 'Physical exercise predicts social competence and general well-being in Chinese children 10 to 15 years old: A preliminary study', *Child Indicators Research*, 11(6), pp. 1935–49.

Tovey, H. (2007a). *Playing outdoors, spaces and places, risk and challenge.* Maidenhead: Open University Press.

ukactive (2017). *School summer holidays driving 'Victorian era' health inequalities among children.* Available at: https://www.ukactive.com/news/school-summer-holidays-driving-victorian-era-health-inequalities-among-children/.

Van den Bosch, M. (2017). *Natural environments, health and wellbeing.* Available at: http://environmentalscience.oxfordre.com/view/10.1093/acrefore/9780199389414.001.0001/acrefore-9780199389414-e-333.

Vio, F., Yañez, M., González, C. G., Fretes, G. and Salinas, J. (2018). 'Teachers' self-perception of their dietary behavior and needs to teach healthy eating habits in the school', *Journal of Health Psychology*, 23(8), pp. 1019–27.

Von Hippel, P. T. and Workman, J. (2016). 'From kindergarten through second grade, U.S. children's obesity prevalence grows only during summer vacations', *Obesity – A Research Journal*, 24(11), pp. 2296–300.

Wang, O. and Zuccollo, J. (2020). *The wellbeing of the school workforce in England.* Available at: https://epi.org.uk/publications-and-research/wellbeing-school-workforce/ (accessed 28 September 2020).

Ward, Z. J., Long, M. W., Resch, S. C., Giles, C. M., Cradock, A. L. and Gortmaker, S. L. (2017). 'Simulation of growth trajectories of childhood obesity into adulthood', *The New England Journal of Medicine*, 377, pp. 2145–53.

Welsh Government (2018). *National survey for Wales 2017–18: Population health – Lifestyle.* Available at: https://gov.wales/docs/statistics/2018/180627-national-survey-2017-18-population-health-lifestyle-en.pdf.

Westergaard, J. and Bainbridge, A. (2014). *Supporting teachers in their role: Making the case for formal supervision in the workplace.* Available at: http://www.consider-ed.org.uk/supporting-teachers-in-their-role-making-the-case-for-formal-supervision-in-the-workplace/.

World Health Organization (2018a). *Physical activity and adults.* Available at: https://www.who.int/dietphysicalactivity/factsheet_adults/en/.

World Health Organization (2018b). 'Mental health: Strengthening our response'. Available at: https://www.who.int/news-room/fact-sheets/detail/mental-health-strengthening-our-response.

World Health Organization (2019). *World Health Organization Constitution'.* Available at: https://www.who.int/about/who-we-are/constitution.

Chapter 4 Child Development

Department for Education (2014). *The national curriculum in England. Framework document.* Available at: https://assets.publishing.service.gov.uk/government/uploads/system/uploads/attachment_data/file/381344/Master_final_national_curriculum_28_Nov.pdf (accessed 21 February 2019).

Department for the Environment, Food and Rural Affairs, European Centre for Environment and Human Health and University of Exeter (2017). *Evidence statement on the links between natural environments and human health*. Available at: https://beyondgreenspace.files.wordpress.com/2017/03/evidence-statement-on-the-links-between-natural-environments-and-human-health1.pdf (accessed 22 September 2018).

Dillon, J. and Dickie, I. (2012). *Learning in the natural environment: Review of social and economic benefits and barriers*. Natural England Commissioned Reports, Number 092. Available at: http://publications.naturalengland.org.uk/publication/1321181 (accessed 26 January 2019).

Doherty, J. and Hughes, M. (2009). *Child development: Theory and practice 0–11*. Harlow: Pearson Education.

Gilchrist, M., Passy, R., Waite, S., Blackwell, I., Edwards-Jones, A., Lewis, J. and Hunt, A. (2017a). *Natural connections demonstration project, 2012–2016: Analysis of the key evaluation questions part 1*, Natural England Commissioned Reports, Number 215 Annex 1. Available at: http://publications.naturalengland.org.uk/publication/6636651036540928 (accessed 2 February 2019).

Gilchrist, M., Passy, R., Waite, S., Blackwell, I., Edwards-Jones, A., Lewis, J. and Hunt, A. (2017b). *Natural connections demonstration project, 2012–2016: Analysis of the key evaluation questions part 2*, Natural England Commissioned Reports, Number 215 Annex 1. Available at: http://publications.naturalengland.org.uk/publication/6636651036540928 (accessed 2 February 2019).

Gill, T. (2014). 'The benefits of children's engagement with nature: A systematic literature review', *Children, Youth and Environments*, 24(2), pp. 10–34.

Gutman, L. and Schoon, I. (2013). *The impact of non-cognitive skills on outcomes for young people: Literature review*, Education Endowment Foundation. Available at: https://educationendowmentfoundation.org.uk/public/files/Publications/EEF_Lit_Review_Non-CognitiveSkills.pdf (accessed 2 February 2019).

HM Government (2011). *The natural choice: Securing the value of nature*. Available at: https://www.gov.uk/government/publications/the-natural-choice-securing-the-value-of-nature (accessed 26 January 2019).

Knight, S. (2011). *Forest school for all*. London: Sage.

Littleton, K. (2005). 'Themes and issues', in Ding, S. and Littleton, K. (eds.) *Children's personal and social development*. Milton Keynes: Blackwell and Open University.

Littleton, K. and Miell, D. (2005). 'Children's interactions: Siblings and peers', in Ding, S. and Littleton, K. (eds.) *Children's personal and social development*. Milton Keynes: Blackwell and Open University.

Louv, R. (2008). *Last child in the woods: Saving our children from nature-deficit disorder*. New York: Algonquin Books of Chapel Hill.

Marketing, E. (2009). *Report to Natural England on childhood and nature: A survey on changing relationships with nature across generations*. Available at: http://publications.naturalengland.org.uk/publication/5853658314964992 (accessed 19 February 2019).

Moll, L., Amanti, C., Neff, D. and Gonzalez, N. (1992). 'Funds of knowledge for teaching: Using a qualitative approach to connect homes and classrooms', *Theory into Practice*, 31(2), pp. 132–41.

Page, A., Bremner, M. and Passy, R. (2017). 'School gardens and the school food plan: Contributing to a culture of healthy living', in Waite, S. (ed.) *Children learning outside from birth to eleven*. 2nd edn. London: Sage, pp. 233–45.

Passy, R., Reed, F. and Morris, M. (2010). *Impact of school gardening on learning: Final report for the Royal Horticultural Society*. Available at: https://www.nfer.ac.uk/impact-of-school-gardening-on-learning (accessed 2 February 2019).

Rickinson, M., Hunt, A., Rogers, J. and Dillon, J. (2012). *School leader and teacher insights into learning outside the classroom in natural environments*, Natural England Commissioned Reports, Number 097. Available at: http://publications.naturalengland.org.uk/publication/1989824 (accessed 2 February 2019).

Waite, S., Passy, R., Gilchrist, M., Hunt, A. and Blackwell, I. (2016). *Natural Connections Demonstration Project, 2012–2016: Final Report*, Natural England Commissioned Reports, Number 215. Available at: http://publications.naturalengland.org.uk/publication/6636651036540928 (accessed 2 February 2019).

Woodhead, M. (2006). 'Children and development', in Oates, J., Wood, C. and Grayson, A. (eds.) *Psychological development and early childhood*. Milton Keynes: Blackwell and Open University.

Chapter 5 Technology Education

Akcaoglu, M. and Koehler, M. J. (2014). 'Cognitive outcomes from the Game-Design and Learning (GDL) after-school program', *Computers and Education*, 75, pp. 72–81.

Autor, D. H., Levy, F. and Murnane, R. J. (2003). 'The skill content of recent technological change: An empirical exploration'. *The Quarterly Journal of Economics*, 118(4): 1279–333.

Barthes, R. (1972). *Mythologies. 1957*. Translated by Lavers, A. New York: Hill and Wang.

Belshaw, D. (2014). *The essential elements of digital literacies*. [Pdf] Self-published. Available at: https://gumroad.com/l/digilit (accessed 2 February 2020).

Bronfenbrenner, U. (1977). 'Towards an ecology of human development', *American Psychologist*, 32, pp. 513–31.

Bruner, J.S. (1966). *Toward a theory of instruction*. Cambridge, MA: Harvard University Press.

Campbell, C. and Walsh, C. (2017). 'Introducing the "new" digital literacy of coding in the early years', *Practical Literacy: The Early and Primary Years*, 22(3), p. 10.

Clark-Wilson, A. and Mostert, I. (2016). 'Teaching and learning mathematics with technology', in Hopkins, C., Anghileri, J. and Gage, J. (eds.) *AIMSSEC maths teacher support series: Mathematical thinking in the lower secondary classroom*. Cambridge: Cambridge University Press, pp. 173–85.

Cunningham, W. F. (2019). *Assistive technology integration for student with speech and language impairments: A mixed method study doctoral dissertation*, Wayne State University ProQuest Dissertations Publishing, 10974787.

DFE (2013). 'Computing programmes of study: Key stages 1 and 2'. Available at: https://www.gov.uk/government/publications/national-curriculum-in-england-computing-programmes-of-study (accessed 2 February 2020).

Du, Y., Abbas, H., Taraman, S., Segar, S. and Bischoff, N. (2019). 'In-home speech and language screening for young children: A proof-of-concept study using interactive mobile storytime', *AMIA Summits on Translational Science Proceedings*, p. 722.

Gabler, N. (2011). 'The Elusive Big Idea', *Sunday Review, The New York Times*, 13 August. Available at: https://www.nytimes.com/2011/08/14/opinion/sunday/the-elusive-big-idea.html (Accessed 29 September 2020).

Gilchrist, A. (2016). *Introducing industry 4.0. in industry 4.0*. Berkeley, CA: Apress.

Harlen, W. and Qualter, W. (2018). *The teaching of science in primary schools*. 7th edn. Abingdon: Routledge.

Heafner, T. L. and Massey, D. (2019). 'Situated word inquiry: Supporting inquiry and language-rich environments through technology-mediated, contextualized word learning', *History Teacher*, 52(3), pp. 441–60.

Hoffmann, D. L., Standish, C. D., García-Diez, M., Pettitt, P. B., Milton, J. A., Zilhão, J., Alcolea-González, J. J., Cantalejo-Duarte, P., Collado, H., De Balbín, R. and Lorblanchet, M. (2018). 'U–Th dating of carbonate crusts reveals Neanderthal origin of Iberian cave art', *Science*, 359(6378), pp. 912–15.

Keighrey, C., Flynn, R., Murray, S. and Murray, N. (2017), 'A QoE evaluation of immersive augmented and virtual reality speech and language assessment applications', *In 2017 Ninth International Conference on Quality of Multimedia Experience (QoMEX)* (pp. 1–6). IEEE.

Kress, G. and Leeuwen, V. (2006). *Reading images: The grammar of visual design*. 2nd edn. London: Routledge.

Kwon, K., Ottenbreit-Leftwich, A. T., Sari, A. R., Khlaif, Z., Zhu, M., Nadir, H. and Gok, F. (2019). 'Teachers' self-efficacy matters: Exploring the integration of mobile computing device in middle schools', *TechTrends*, 63(6), pp. 682–92.

McAfee, A. (2015). 'The great decoupling', Interview with Eric Brynjolfsson and Andrew McAfee. Interviewed by Amy Bernstein and Anand Raman for *The Harvard Business Review*, June, pp. 66–74.

McDougall, J. (2013). 'Creativity v. technology', *Journal of Media Practice*, 14(1), pp. 3–4.

McFarlane, A. (2014). *Authentic learning for the digital generation: Realising the potential of technology in the classroom*. Abingdon: Routledge.

OECD (2003). *PISA 2003 assessment framework: Mathematics, reading, science and problem solving knowledge and skills*. Available at: http://www.oecd.org/education/school/programmeforinternationalstudentassessmentpisa/33694881.pdf (accessed 10 January 2020).

OECD (2019). *What do we know about children and technology?* Available at: https://www.oecd.org/education/ceri/Booklet-21st-century-children.pdf (accessed 10 January 2020).

Orben, A. (2020). 'Teenagers, screens and social media: A narrative review of reviews and key studies', *Social Psychiatry and Psychiatric Epidemiology*, 55, pp. 407–14. DOI: 10.1007/s00127-019-01825-4.

Pahl, K. (2002). 'Ephemera, mess and miscellaneous piles: Texts and practices in families', *Journal of Early Childhood Literacy*, 2(2), pp. 145–66.

Parry, B., Burnett, C. and Merchant, G. (eds.) (2016). *Literacy, media, technology: Past, present and future*. London: Bloomsbury.

Parsons, L. (2012). *Back to learning*. Markham, Pembroke Publishers Limited.

Payler, J., Wood, E., Georgeson, J., Davis, G., Jarvis, P., Rose, J., Gilbert, L., Hood, P., Mitchell, H. and Chesworth, L. (2017) *BERA-TACTYC early childhood research review 2003–2017*. London: BERA.

Plato (1925). *Phaedrus* in Plato. Translated by Fowler, H. N. Cambridge, MA: Harvard University Press.

Plowman, L., Stevenson, S., Stephen, C. and McPake, J. (2012). 'Preschool children's learning with technology at home', *Computers and Education*, 59, pp. 30–7.

Qualter, A. (2011). 'Using ICT in teaching and learning Science', in Harlen, W. (ed.) *ASE guide to primary science education*. Hatfield: Association for Science Education, pp. 61–68

Quinlan, O. (2015). *Young digital makers*. London: Nesta.

Rogers, E. M. (2003). *Diffusion of innovations*. 5th edn. New York: Free Press.

Savage, M., Barnett, A. and Rogers, M. (2017) *Technology-enhanced Learning in the Early Years Foundation Stage*. Northwich: Northwich: Critical Publishing.

Tate, T. P. (2018). *Prior technology exposure, keyboard/mouse activity, and writing achievement: Analysis of the 2011 National Assessment of Educational Progress Writing Assessment*. eScholarship, University of California.

White, D. S. and Le Cornu, A. (2011). 'Visitors and residents: A new typology for online engagement', *First Monday*, 16(9). Available at: https://firstmonday.org/ojs/index.php/fm/article/download/3171/3049 (accessed 6 October 2020).

WHO (2019). *To grow up healthy, children need to sit less and play more*. Available at: https://www.who.int/news-room/detail/24-04-2019-to-grow-up-healthy-children-need-to-sit-less-and-play-more (accessed 3 February 2020).

Zipke, M. (2017). 'Pre-schoolers explore interactive storybook apps: The effect on word recognition and story comprehension', *Education and Information Technologies*, 22(4), pp. 1695–712.

Chapter 6 Listening to Children

Arnold, C. (2010). *Understanding schemas and emotion in early childhood*. London: Sage.

Athey, C. (2009). *Extending thought in young children: A parent–teacher partnership*. London: Sage.

Campbell-Barr, V. (2015). 'The research, policy and practice triangle in early childhood education and care', in Parker-Rees, R. and Leeson, C. (eds.) *Early childhood studies*. Exeter: Learning Matters, pp. 243–63.

Campbell-Barr, V. (2019). *Professional knowledge and skills in the early years*. London: Sage.

Campbell-Barr, V. and Leeson, C. (2016). *Quality and leadership in the early years*. London: Sage.

Clark, A. and Moss, P. (2011). *Listening to young children the mosaic approach*. 2nd edn. London: National Children's Bureau.

Dahlberg, G. and Moss, P. (2005). *Ethics and politics in early childhood education*. London: RoutledgeFalmer.

Dahlberg, G., Pence, A. and Moss, P. (2013). *Beyond quality in early childhood education and care: Languages of evaluation*. Classic edn. London: Routledge.

Davies, B. (2014). *Listening to children, being and becoming*. Oxon: Routledge.

Department for Education (2014). *Statutory framework for the early years foundation stage (EYFS)*. London: Crown Copyright.

Friere, P. (1996). *Pedagogy of the oppressed*. London: Penguin.

Georgeson, J. (2018). 'Ways of working with two year olds', in Georgeson, J. and Campbell-Barr, V. (eds.) *Places for two-year-olds in the early years: Supporting learning and development.*. London: Routledge, pp. 63–74.

Goldschmied, E. and Jackson, S. (1994). *People under Three: Young children in day care*. London: Routledge

Heckman, J. (2000). *Invest in the very young*. Chicago, IL: Ounce of Prevention Fund and the University of Chicago Harris School of Public Policy Studies.

Hendrick, H. (1997). 'Constructions and reconstructions of British childhood: An interpretative survey, 1800 to the present', in James, A., and Prout, A. (eds.) *Constructing and reconstructing childhood: Contemporary issues in the sociological study of childhood*, London: Routledge Falmer, pp. 33–60.

Hevey, D. (2012). 'Introduction: Critical perspectives on early years policy-making', in Miller, L. and Hevey, D. (eds.) *Policy issues in the early years*. London: Sage, pp. 1–10.

Laevers, F., Moons, J. and Declercq, B. (2012). *A process oriented monitoring system for the early years (POMS)*. Leuven, Belgium: CEGO Publishers.

Lee, N. (2003). *Childhood and society: Growing up in an age of uncertainty*. Buckingham: Open University Press.

Lee, W. (2015). 'Essence of Te Whāriki', *Pen Green Symposium*, Nothamptonshire. 19 September.

Lloyd, E. (2014). 'Co-producing early years policy in England under the Coalition Government', *Management in Education*, 28(4), pp. 130–7.

Malaguzzi, L. (1993). 'Your Image of the child: Where teaching begins', *Unknown*, Reggio Emilia. Available at: https://www.reggioalliance.org/downloads/malaguzzi:ccie:1994.pdf (accessed 20 April 2020).

Malaguzzi, L. (1994). www.reggiochildren.it/2011/09/2617/notizia-di-prova-consulenza/.

Moss, P. (2014a). 'Early childhood policy in England 1997–2013: Anatomy of a missed opportunity', *International Journal of Early Years Education*, 22(4), pp. 346–58. DOI: 10.1080/09669760.2014.968533.

Moss, P. (2014b). *Transformative change and real utopias in early childhood education: A story of democracy, experimentation and potentiality*. Abingdon, Oxon: Routledge.

Nutbrown, C. and Clough, P. (2014). *Early Childhood Education, History, Phiosphy and Experience*. London: Sage.

Nyland, B., Ferris, J. and Dunn, L. (2008). 'Mindful hands, gestures as language: Listening to children', *Early Years: An International Research Journal*, 28(1), pp. 73–80.

Palaiologou, I. (2014). '"Do we hear what children want to say?" Ethical praxis when choosing research tools with children under five', *Early Child Development and Care*, 184(5), pp. 689–705.

Penn, H. (2012). 'Shaping the future: How human capital arguments about investment in early childhood are being (mis)used in poor countries', in Yelland, N. (ed.) *Contemporary perspective on early childhood education*. Maidenhead: Open University Press, pp. 49–65.

Podmore, V., May, H. and Carr, M. (2001). 'The "child's questions": Programme evaluation with Te Whāriki using "Teaching Stories"', *NZCER, Early Childhood Folio (ECF)*, 5(6).

Robinson, K. and Aronica, L. (2014). *Creative schools, revolutionizing education from the ground up*. London: Penguin Random House.

Rubin, H. J. and Rubin, I. S. (2012). *Qualitative Interviewing, The art of hearing data*. London: Sage.

Siraj-Blatchford, I., Sylva, K., Muttock, S., Gildern, R. and Bell, D. (2002). *Researching effective pedagogy in the early years: Research report no. 356*. Department for Education. London: Queens Printer.

Stewart, N. (2011). *How children learn: The characteristics of effective early learning*. London: British Association for Early Childhood Education.

Tartt, D. (2013). *The Goldfinch*. London: Abacus.

Tovey, H. (2007b). *Playing outdoors, spaces and places, risk and challenge*. Berks: Open University Press.

Trevarthen, C. (2013). *Artful learning makes sense, articles for the 90th anniversary of early education*. London: British Association for Early Childhood Education. Available at: https://www.early-education.org.uk/sites/default/files/90th-article%20 1-Trevarthen.pdf.

Chapter 7 Professional Relationships and Collaboration

Ainsworth, M. D. S. (1991). 'Attachment and other affectional bonds across the life-cycle', in Parkes, C. M., Stevenson-Hinde, J. and Marris, P. (eds.) *Attachment across the life cycle*. London: Routledge, pp. 33-51.

Ainsworth, M. D. S., Blehar, M. C., Waters, E. and Walls, S. (1978). *Patterns of attachment*. Hillsdale, NJ: Lawrence Erlbaum Associates, Inc.

Beek, G. J., Zuiker, I. and Zwart, R. C. (2018). 'Exploring mentors' roles and feedback strategies to analyse the quality of mentoring dialogues', *Teaching and Teacher Education*, 78, pp. 15–27.

Bourdieu, P. and Wacquant, L.P.D. (1992). *An invitation to reflexive sociology*. Chicago, IL: University of Chicago Press.

Bowlby, J. (1969). *Attachment. Attachment and loss: Vol. 1*. New York: Basic Books.

Brayne, H., Carr, H. and Goosey, D. (2015). *Law for social workers*. Oxford: Oxford University Press.

Bronfenbrenner, U. (1979a). *The ecology of human development*. 1st edn. Cambridge, MA: Harvard University Press.

Children's Society (2019). *The good childhood report*. Available at: https://www.childrenssociety.org.uk/sites/default/files/the_good_childhood_report_2019.pdf.

DeLuca, C., Bolden, B. and Chan, J. (2017). 'Systemic professional learning through collaborative inquiry: Examining teachers' perspectives', *Teaching and Teacher Education* 67, pp. 67–78.

DfE (2018a). *Get into teaching – School direct*. Available at: https://getintoteaching.education.gov.uk/explore-my-options/teacher-training-routes/school-led-training/school-direct.

DfE (2018b). *Mental health and wellbeing Provision in Schools*. Available at: https://assets.publishing.service.gov.uk/government/uploads/system/uploads/attachment_data/file/747709/Mental_health_and_wellbeing_provision_in_schools.pdf (accessed 26 October 2019)

DfE (2019a). *Keeping children safe in education: For schools and colleges*. Available at: https://assets.publishing.service.gov.uk/government/uploads/system/uploads/attachment_data/file/835733/Keeping_children_safe_in_education_2019.pdf (accessed 26 October 2019).

DfE (2019b). *Relationships Education, Relationships and Sex Education (RSE) and Health Education Statutory guidance for governing bodies, proprietors, head teachers, principals, senior leadership teams, teachers*. Available at: https://assets.publishing.service.gov.uk/government/uploads/system/uploads/attachment_data/file/805781/Relationships_Education__Relationships_and_Sex_Education__RSE__and_Health_Education.pdf (accessed 22 October 2019).

Eraut, M. (2007). 'Learning from other people in the workplace', *Oxford Review of Education*, 33(4), pp. 403–22.

Gardner, H. (1999). *Intelligence reframed. Multiple intelligences for the 21st century*. New York: Basic Books.

Garelli, S. (2017). *If you want to lead people, you have to enter their world Lessons from Warren Bennis, Leo Varadkar, Brexit and Trump*. CH-1001 Lausanne: IMD Switzerland. Available at: https://www.imd.org/research-knowledge/articles/if-you-want-to-lead-people-you-have-to-enter-their-world/.

Gibbs, B. (2017). *It takes two (or more) to tango ... A relational guide to dating for schools*. Available at: http://relationalschools.org/wp-content/uploads/2017/08/A-Relational-Guide-to-Dating-for-Schools-1.pdf.

Gibbs, S. and Bodman, S. (2014). *Phonological assessment and battery – Primary second edition (PhAB2)*. Brentford, London: GLS Assessment.

Goleman, D. (2006). *Emotional intelligence*. Ealing: Bantam.

Hargreaves, A. and Fullan, M. (2013). 'The power of professional capital' 8 JSD, www.learningforward.org, June, 34(3). Available at: http://www.michaelfullan.ca/wp-content/uploads/2013/08/JSD-Power-of-Professional-Capital.pdf.

Howe, D. (2011). *Attachment across the lifecourse*. Basingstoke: Palgrave Macmillan.

Loe, R. (2014). *Building a case for relational reform in Education: Towards a relational pedagogy*. Available at: https://berarespectingchildren.wordpress.com/2014/10/16/building-a-case-for-relational-reform-in-education-towards-a-relational-pedagogy/.

McConnell, N., Thomas, E., Bosher, A. and Cotmore, R. (2019). *Early support for military-connected families: Evaluation of services at NSPCC military sites*. London: NSPCC.

Music, G. (2017). *'Middle childhood, siblings and peers', Nurturing Natures – Attachment and children's emotional, socio-cultural and brain development*. 2nd edn. London: Routledge.

Noddings, N. (2012). 'The caring relation in teaching', *Oxford Review of Education*, 38(6), pp. 771–81.

Reeves, J. and Le Mare, L. (2017). 'Supporting teachers in relational pedagogy and social emotional education: A qualitative exploration', *The International Journal of Emotional Education*, 9(1), pp. 85–98.

Relationships Foundation (2019). *Teachers get by with a little help from their friends*. Available at: https://relationshipsfoundation.org/events/in-the-news/teachers-get-by-with-a-little-help-from-their-friends/.

Seldon, A. (2009). *Trust. How we lost it and how to get it back*. London: Biteback Publishing Ltd.

Vangrieken, K., Grosemans, I., Dochy, F. and Kyndt, E. (2017). 'Teacher autonomy and collaboration: A paradox? Conceptualising and measuring teacher's autonomy and collaborative attitude', *Teaching and Teacher Education*, 67, pp. 302–15.

Chapter 8 Resilience, Reflection and Reflexivity

Argyris, C. and Schön, D. A. (1974). *Theory in practice: Increasing professional effectiveness*. San Francisco, CA: Jossey-Bass.

Barry, H. (2018). *Emotional resilience: How to safeguard your mental health*. London: Orion Spring.

Bronfenbrenner, U. (1979). *The ecology of human development*. London: Harvard University Press.

Brookfield, S. (1995). *Becoming a critically reflective teacher*. San Francisco, CA: Jossey-Bass.

Charteris, J. and Smith, J. (2017). 'Sacred and secret stories in professional knowledge landscapes: Learner agency in teacher professional learning', *Reflective Practice*, 18(5), pp. 600–12.

Dewey, J. (1933). *How we think: A restatement of the relation of reflective thinking to the educative process*. Boston, MA: Houghton Mifflin.

Dewey, J. (1938). *Experience and Education*. New York: Collier Books.

Dweck, C. S. (2007). *Mindset: The new psychology of success*. New York: Ballantine.

Eraut, M. (1994). *Developing professional knowledge and competence*. London: Falmer Press.

Eraut, M. (2000). 'Non-formal learning and tacit knowledge in professional work', *British Journal of Educational Psychology*, 70(1), pp. 113–36.

Eraut, M. (2002). *Developing professional knowledge and competence*. 2nd edn. London: Falmer Press.

Eraut, M. (2004). 'The emotional dimension of learning', *Learning in Health and Social Care*, 3, pp. 1–4.

Feucht, F., Brownlee, J. and Schraw, G. (2017). 'Moving beyond reflection: Reflexivity and epistemic cognition in teaching and teacher education', *Educational Psychologist*, 52(4), pp. 234–41.

Finlayson, A. (2015). 'Reflective practice: Has it really changed over time?', *Reflective Practice*, 16(6), pp. 717–30.

Fook, J. (1999b). 'Reflexivity as Method', in Daly, J., Kellehear, A. and Willis, F. (eds.) *Annual review of Health Social Sciences*, 9, pp. 11–20.

Fook, J. and Askeland, G. (2006). 'The "critical" in critical reflection', in White, S., Fook, J. and Gardner, F. (eds.) *Critical reflection in health and social care*. Maidenhead: Open University Press/McGraw-Hill Education, p. 45.

Fook, J. and Gardner, F. (2007). *Practising critical reflection – A resources handbook*. Berkshire: Open University Press.

Goleman, D. (1995). *Emotional intelligence*. New York: Bantam Books.

Hargreaves, A. (2000). 'Mixed emotions: Teachers' perceptions of their interactions with students', *Teaching and Teacher Education*, 16(8), pp. 811–26.

Harnett, J. (2012). 'Reducing discrepancies between teachers' espoused theories and theories-in-use: An action research model of reflective professional development', *Educational Action Research*, 20(3), pp. 367–84.

Hochschild, R. (1983). *The managed heart: The commercialization of human feeling*. Berkley: University of California Press.

Johns, C. (1995). 'Framing learning through reflection within Carper's fundamental ways of knowing in nursing', *Journal of Advanced Nursing*, 22, pp. 226–34.

Kemmis, S. (2006). 'Participatory action research and the public sphere', *Educational Action Research*, 14(4), pp. 459–76.

Kramer, M. (2018). 'Promoting teachers' agency: Reflective practice as transformative disposition', *Reflective Practice: International and Multidisciplinary Perspectives*, 19(2), pp. 211–24.

Leithwood, K., Steinbach, R. and Ryan, S. (1997). 'Leadership and team learning in secondary schools', *School Leadership and Management*, 17(3), pp. 303–26.

Luther, S., Cicchetti, D. and Becker, B. (2000). 'The construct of resilience: A critical evaluation and guidelines for future work', *Child Development*, 71, pp. 543–62.

McCotter, S. (2001). 'Collaborative groups as professional development', *Teaching and Teacher Education*, 17, pp. 685–704.

Mezirow, J. (1990). *Fostering critical reflection in adulthood: A guide to transformative and emancipatory learning*. San Francisco, CA: Jossey-Bass.

Mezirow, J. (1998). 'On critical reflection', *Adult Education Quarterly*, 48(3), pp. 185–98.

Nias, J. (1998). 'Why teachers need their colleagues: A developmental perspective', in Hargreaves, A., Lieberman, A., Fullan, M. and Hopkins, D. (eds.) *International handbook of educational change*. London: Kluwer, p. 1257.

Pollard, A. (2019). *Reflective teaching in schools*. London: Bloomsbury Academic.

Schon, D. (1987). *Educating the reflective practitioner*. San Francisco: Jossey-Bass.

Schön, D. A. (1983). *The reflective practitioner: How professionals think in action*. New York: Basic Books.

Siebert, S. and Costley, C. (2013). 'Conflicting values in reflection on professional practice', *Higher Education, Skills and Work-based Learning*, 3(3), pp. 156–67.

Thompson, N. and Pascal, J. (2011). 'Reflective practice. An existentialist perspective', *Reflective Practice*, 12(1), pp. 15–26.

Thompson, N. and Pascal, J. (2012). 'Developing critically reflective practice', *Reflective Practice*, 13(2), pp. 311–25.

Chapter 9 The Role of the Teacher

Ball, S. J. (2003). 'The teacher's soul and the terrors of performativity', *Journal of Education Policy*, 18(2), pp. 215–28.

Ball, S. J. (2016). 'Neoliberal education? Confronting the slouching beast', *Policy Futures in Education*, 14(8), 1046–59.

Barnett, R. (2000). 'Supercomplexity and the curriculum', *Studies in Higher Education*, 25(3), pp. 255–65.

BERA (2014). *Research and the teaching profession: Building a capacity for a self-improving education system*. Available at: https://www.bera.ac.uk/wp-content/uploads/2013/12/BERA-RSA-Research-Teaching-Profession-FULL-REPORT-for-web.pdf?noredirect=1.

Bradbury, A. and Roberts-Holmes, G. (2018). *The Datafication of primary and early years education*. Abingdon: Routledge.

Broadhead, P. and Burt, A. (2012). *Understanding young children's learning through play: Building playful pedagogies*. Abingdon: Routledge.

Bronfenbrenner, U. (1979c). *The ecology of human development*. Cambridge, MA: Harvard University Press.

Campbell, J. and Neill, J. (1994). *Primary teachers at work*. London: Routledge.

Claxton, G. (1999). *Wise up: The challenge of life-long learning*. London: Bloomsbury.

Coldwell, M. et al. (2017). *Evidence-informed teaching: Evaluation of progress in England*. Available at: https://assets.publishing.service.gov.uk/government/uploads/system/uploads/attachment_data/file/625007/Evidence-informed_teaching_-_an_evaluation_of_progress_in_England.pdf.

Cox, A. and Sykes, G. (2016). *The multiple identities of the reception teacher pedagogy and purpose*. London: Sage.

Dahlberg, G., Moss, P., and Pence, A. (2013). *Beyond Quality in Early Childhood Education and Care: Languages of evaluation*. Abingdon: Routledge.

Department for Education (DfE) (2015). *Workload challenge: Analysis of teacher consultation responses*, February 2015. London: DfE.

Department for Education (DfE) (2017). *Teacher workload survey 2016*. London: DfE.

Department for Education (DfE) (2019a). *Reducing teacher workload*. Available at: https://www.gov.uk/government/collections/reducing-school-workload.

Department for Education (DfE) (2019b). *Early years foundation stage reforms. Government consultation*. Available at: https://www.gov.uk/government/consultations/early-years-foundation-stage-reforms.

Edwards, C., Gandini, L. and Forman, G. (eds.) (1998). *The hundred languages of children: The Reggio Emilia approach – Advanced reflections*. 2nd edn. New Jersey, NJ: Ablex Publishing.

Ewing, R. and Manual, J. (2005). *Retaining quality early career teachers in the profession: New teacher narratives*. Available at: https://www.researchgate.net/publication/284612572_Retaining_quality_early_career_teachers_in_the_profession_New_teacher_narratives/download.

Festinger, L. (1962). *A theory of cognitive dissonance* (Vol. 2). Stanford, CA: Stanford University Press.

Foster, D. (2018). *Teacher recruitment and retention in England*, Briefing Paper No. 72222, December. Available at: http://researchbriefings.files.parliament.uk/documents/CBP-7222/CBP-7222.pdf.

Geiger, T. and Pivovarova, M. (2018). 'The effects of working conditions on teacher retention', *Teachers and Teaching*, pp. 604–25.

General Teaching Council for England (2006). *Research engaged professional practice*. London: NFER.

Goleman, D. (1996). *Emotional intelligence: Why it can matter more than IQ*. London: Bloomsbury.

Griffin, A. (2008). '"Designer doctors": Professional identity and a portfolio career as a general practice educator', *Education for Primary Care*, 19(4), pp. 355–9.

Gu, Q. (2014). 'How do people become effective teachers?', in Pollard, A. (ed.) *Readings for reflective teaching in schools*. 2nd edn. London: Bloomsbury, pp. 4–6.

Handy, C. (1993). *Understanding organizations*. Oxford, UK: : Penguin.

Hargreaves, A. (1998). 'The emotional practice of teaching', *Teaching and Teacher Education*, 14(8), pp. 835–54.

Hargreaves, A. (2003). *Teaching in the knowledge society: Education in the age of insecurity*. London: Teachers College Press.

Löfström, E. and Poom-Valickis, K. (2013). 'Beliefs about teaching: Persistent or malleable? A longitudinal study of prospective student teachers' beliefs', *Teaching and Teacher Education*, 35, pp. 104–13.

Lynch, S., Worth, J., Bamford, S. and Wespieser, K. (2016). *Engaging teachers: NFER analysis of teacher retention*. Slough: NFER.

Moyles, J. (2001). 'Passion, paradox and professionalism in early years education', *Early Years*, 21(2), pp. 81–95.

Moyles, J. and Adams, S. (2001). *Statements of entitlement to play. A framework for playful teaching.* Buckingham: Open University Press.

OECD (1996). *The knowledge-based economy.* Available at: http://www.oecd.org/officialdocuments/publicdisplaydocumentpdf/?cote=OCDE/GD%2896%29102&docLanguage=En.

Ofsted (2019). *The education inspection framework.* Available at: https://assets.publishing.service.gov.uk/government/uploads/system/uploads/attachment_data/file/801429/Education_inspection_framework.pdf.

Osgood, J. (2010). 'Reconstructing professionalism in ECEC: The case for the "critically reflective emotional professional"', *Early Years*, 30(2), pp. 119–33.

Page, J. (2011). 'Do mothers want professional careers to love their babies?', *Journal of Early Childhood Research*, 9(3), pp. 310–23.

Piaget, J. (1929). *The child's conception of the world.* London: Routledge and Kegan Paul.

Pillen, M. T., Den Brock, P. J. and Beijard, D. (2013). 'Profiles and change in beginning teachers' professional identity tensions', *Teaching and Teacher Education*, 34, pp. 86–97.

Pollard, A. (2014). *Reflective teaching in schools.* 4th edn. London: Bloomsbury.

Roberts-Holmes, G. (2014). 'The "datafication" of early years pedagogy: "If the teaching is good, the data should be good and if there's bad teaching, there is bad data"', *Journal of Education Policy*, 30 (3), pp. 1–13.

Sachs, J. (2016). 'Teacher professionalism, why are we still talking about it?', *Teachers and Teaching: Theory and Practice*, 22(4), pp. 413–25.

Santry, C. (2018). 'At some point, we have to employ a moral compass', *The Times Educational Supplement*, 5247, p. 16.

Schaefer, L., Long, J. S. and Clandinin, D. J. (2012). 'Questioning the research on early career teacher attrition and retention', *Alberta Journal of Educational Research*, 58, pp. 106–21.

Skattebol, J., Adamson, E. and Woodrow, C. (2016). 'Revisioning professionalism from the periphery', *Early Years*, 36(2), pp. 116–31.

Steinberg, S. and Kincheloe, J. (1998). *Students as researchers – Creating classrooms that matter.* London: Falmer Press.

Vygotsky, L. (1978). *Mind in society. The development of higher psychological processes.* Harvard: Harvard University Press.

Walker, M., Nelson, J., Bradshaw, S. and Brown, C. (2019). *Teacher's engagement with research: What do we know? A research briefing.* Available at: https://educationendowmentfoundation.org.uk/public/files/Evaluation/Teachers_engagement_with_research_Research_Brief_JK.pdf.

Webster, F. (2006). *Theories of the information society.* 3rd edn. Abingdon: Routledge.

Wyse, D. and Torrance, H. (2009). 'The development and consequences of national curriculum assessment for primary education in England', *Educational Research*, 51(2), pp. 213–28.

INDEX